MANAHOLIC

A JOURNEY TO RECOVERING ME

LORILYN B. ALDEN

E-book ISBN: 979-8-9922971-1-9

Print ISBN: 979-8-9922971-0-2

Audiobook ISBN: 979-8-9922971-2-6

Cover design by BrookeFischer.com.

Burned Haystack Dating Method® used by permission.

Published by Souls Work Publishing

CONTENTS

MANAHOLIC

Note to Readers

This book contains sensitive content related to trauma, eating disorders, and disordered eating and may not be appropriate for everyone. While this book shares insights and inspiration, it is for self-growth purposes only and is not a substitute for professional therapy, counseling, or medical advice.

If you or someone you know is struggling, please reach out to one of the resources below: Survivors to Thrivers, help and support for abusive relationships and trauma; Eating Disorder Foundation, offers peer mentoring and support groups; Project Heal, which offers financial assistance in obtaining eating disorder treatment; Eating Disorder Hope, an online community for support, information, and hope; the Crisis Text Line, to connect online with a trained volunteer; or the Crisis Hotline, which can also be reached by dialing 988. Please note these resources are not a substitute for medical or mental health advice. Should you be in a life-threatening situation, immediately notify your local authorities.

ACKNOWLEDGMENTS AND GRATITUDE

Thank you for taking the time to read my book. I avoided sharing the intimate details of my life for a long time out of fear of being judged and shamed and from reliving the trauma, but an inner voice kept nagging me, encouraging me to share my stories. My life's mission is to be transparent and transform myself and others through my spoken and written words. My vision is a world where women can speak their truth and have the financial freedom to live lives aligned with their authentic selves. How can I fulfill my life's purpose unless I am willing to share my experiences and lessons?

Although this book is based on a true story, some names have been changed to protect the innocent and the not so innocent. Even though I have some concerns for myself and my safety, the decision was made primarily to protect my sons. It is my humble request that you honor their privacy. I am most grateful for their loving support and understanding of my need to express my truth. I am thankful for the honor and privilege of being their mom on this journey. They are my inspiration for my deep work and for continuing to interrupt negative generational behaviors.

During the writing process of this book, I learned many things about myself. I feared being judged, but it was I who was the most critical. I always thought I was weak and gave in to my addiction to men quickly. But now, in retrospect, I see myself as resilient and how I would not settle—how I was still moving forward! And I never gave up, even when I didn't know my self-worth.

I also learned that although I believed for most of my life that I was alone on this journey of life, that was, in fact, not the truth. I now realize the Universe has always supported me. This book would not even exist without all the angels the Divine put on life's journey with me. Thank you to all my beautiful friends who have become my soul family. Over the years, you have watched me grow, sometimes painfully, but you have always loved me regardless of the lessons I was learning or the adventures I was on. I would not be the woman I am today without every single one of you.

I want to thank my amazing mentors and coaches for guiding, supporting, and giving me the tools to step into my authenticity and fulfill my life purpose. Each one of you provided essential information to my growth and transformation.

To all my angels who served as book publishing advisors. Thank you for willfully and generously sharing your knowledge with me as I stumbled my way through this amazing and sometimes challenging opportunity of publishing. The actual production of this book is because of your guidance, patience, and support.

There is a saying that it takes a village, which, as you can tell from my gratitude so far, is true, but I have a special thank-you to the strong women who played an integral part in this creation. For years, Nancy and I talked about working together for me to get a book out, and that has come to fruition with the birth of *Manaholic*. Nancy didn't just take on the role of developmental editor, but she held my hand through the entire process. And trust me, there were some downright awful days along the way, but she never gave up on me and always got me back on purpose. No words can capture the gratitude in my heart for her love and support and how she believed in me on days when I did not believe in myself. Thank you, Nancy.

Then there is Brooke, the cover art designer who answered my crazy email inquiry when I bought a card with her artwork. After getting home, I realized her website was on it and checked her work. Between her beautiful art and her work for social justice, I knew she was the one to design the cover. She truly captured the essence of the message I wanted to convey. The concept behind the artwork for *Manaholic* is about being blinded by a burning desire for love but growing, blossoming, and coming out of the darkness to discover and recover a whole new you. I love the cover art and am so grateful that Brooke shared her talents and collaborated with me. Thank you, Brooke.

And no book would be complete without an outstanding line editor. When I met Annie, she provided a sample of her work for me to consider. The fact that she wanted to make sure that whoever I worked with, whether I chose her or not, maintained my voice made me realize that she was the one to take this project home immediately. Making sure that my voice was heard and honored was my utmost priority. Thank you, Annie.

To learn more about these amazing women of literature, check out the section in the back of the book titled Meet the Tribe.

A special thank-you to my mom and dad for doing the best you could raising me with the tools, knowledge, and experience you had. You were the best people for the job, and I am grateful. I believe you would be proud of me and my work.

Thank you to every man and woman, whether mentioned in this book or not, who allowed me to heal my wounds and evolve into the strong woman I am today.

May every woman reconnect with her voice, know her worth, follow her heart's desires, and live the life she desires.

INTRODUCTION

In the Dark

When we lived in tribes, wisdom from shared experiences was passed down from generation to generation through storytelling. Today, when people who think differently from our norms speak out in our current social environment, they are often met with harsh criticism and judgment. In some instances, our society treats victims of unhealthy or harmful relationships as if they were the perpetrator, leaving them victimized all over again. For this reason, most of us don't share our personal stories and experiences, leaving us to either work through them alone or stuff them so far down into our souls that they impact our health mentally and physically.

Because of our fears, we are left to stand alone in the dark. But think about what happens in the dark. Dangerous mold grows, and cockroaches come out, but in the light, they cannot flourish. What if we started to have open conversations about the mold in our society, how to reduce the spread, and how we treat victims? What if we came together to support each other? Where would the cockroaches scatter off to when the light chases them back into the shadows?

Although I share some of my most embarrassing moments as well as challenging-to-read (and write) chapters about an assault, I did not write this from the place of being a victim. It was written from a place of empowerment. It is about overcoming my addiction and reclaiming my voice. It is about creating a platform to develop transformative conversations in the light and to change our world one conversation at a time.

My Soapbox

If you have experienced healthy relationships during your lifetime so far, please read the following pages with an open mind and do your best not to judge. This request is partially for me, but it is also for the many others who have experienced trauma.

Victims of toxic experiences often stay in unhealthy situations longer than they need to out of fear of judgment or being revictimized all over again should they speak out, which is why many suffer alone in silence.

In January of 2024, I was enrolled in an eight-week course called Spiritual Economics based on the book written by Eric Butterworth. It was taught at a local Science of Mind church. Like most spiritual churches, they believe that we all create our own reality. Being a person who has experienced a lot of traumas over my lifetime, I had a hard time accepting that concept. I was downright pissed off about it when first introduced. How, as a child, could I have created such traumatic experiences? Were they nuts? But if you believe that your soul planned before you were even born what lessons you wanted to learn or what experiences you wanted to have, then there could be truth that we cocreate our life experiences to fulfill our life contracts.

During our classroom discussions, one of the Zoom participants, Maggie, appeared emotionally charged by this belief of creating all our experiences. She told the facilitator that she felt the class should have come with a warning or disclaimer of such beliefs. I assumed she'd taken the class before she realized the principles the church was founded on. As she went back and forth with the instructor, some people attending the class in person started to mumble. Maggie then asked about children who are in abusive situations. How did they create that? That was when another woman in the classroom, Babs, said under her breath but loud enough for me to hear in the back of the room, "When you're a child, you're a victim. When you're an adult, you're a willing participant." I felt my blood boil. Thank goodness the facilitator did an excellent job of deescalating the conversation and then taking it in a different direction.

I can only assume from Maggie's reaction to the concept that she had experienced some abuse. She might not have been ready to ponder the teachings of that spiritual community, or maybe when she was not upset, she could explore that further. But the comment that the women in the room made gnawed at me during the days after. As a communication expert, I am used to having uncomfortable conversations. Because I practice what I teach, I invited her to have a cup of coffee when I was no longer emotionally charged. Trying to have any meaningful conversation while under the influence of our body's chemistry due to emotional reactions is like driving a car under the influence of alcohol or drugs. Nothing good can come of it.

Babs accepted my invitation. We met at a diner and sat outside. We ordered lunch and got to know each other a little better. Babs shared the church's history, as she has been a long-term member. At one point during the lunch I considered not even confronting her with her comment as I was not sure how open she would be to that conversation. I weighed how emotionally draining it might be on me and how I might just be wasting my breath because I noticed a lot of what she was sharing with me sounded somewhat judgmental. As I sat there already feeling emotionally drained, I decided that I would go for it.

I wanted to come from a place of curiosity, so I asked, "Babs, during class, you made a comment about as a child, you're a victim, and as an adult, you are a willing participant. I am just curious as to what you mean by that." She quickly responded, "Oh, you heard that? I thought I said that under my breath." She explained that she was just repeating that quote she had heard before and went on to explain that as a child you don't know any better, but as an adult, you do. I took a deep breath before I asked her if she had ever experienced abuse. I was confident I knew her answer, but I reminded myself to stay open-minded. Then she confirmed my hunch was indeed correct. Babs is one of the fortunate people who had not experienced abuse.

I then asked Babs whether it could be possible that people who grew up in abusive situations consider that to be normal; therefore when they get older, they continue to have the same experience without realizing that it is unhealthy.

Babs had never thought of it that way and, to my pleasant surprise, was open to what I was sharing. I then asked Babs if we could rephrase her statement. I suggested that if she was going to continue to use the quote, would she be willing to modify it to something like: "You are a victim until you have the awareness that you are able to make the choice." I went on to share that if we keep using quotes like the one she recited, it could lead to victims staying in unhealthy situations or relationships out of feeling judged or shamed.

When we have the "you're a willing participant to abuse" mentality, not only do we further disempower victims, but we also empower their perpetrators. The perpetrator wants them to feel alone and scared. Fear is the very thing that keeps predators in control.

I know this, as I have experienced it firsthand many times. Abuse doesn't know age, education level, social or economic status. It can happen to anyone at any point. If you have been lucky not to have had this experience in your lifetime, wherever you are on the journey, I am grateful you haven't had to work through all the emotional baggage it creates. But will you please be curious enough to consider how you would like to be treated by your family, friends, and community if you had been?

Thank you for the consideration and willingness to heal one person at a time. I will step off my soapbox now.

CHAPTER ONE

ADMITTING I HAVE A PROBLEM

I am a manaholic. It has been over a year since I had a date. But in a moment of weakness and feeling sorry for myself because all my single friends now have relationships, I broke down and did something I knew wasn't correct for me: I signed up for a dating site. Again. My desire for male attention was strong, and I found myself powerless to resist going on a date. I accept that I am a recovering manaholic.

I had joked with my friends that male attention was an addiction for me, hence how I came to use the term Manaholic, which means putting the need for male attention above everything else, including my own needs, goals, dreams, children, and friends. I had been so conditioned over my life—in my upbringing and society's narratives of princesses waiting to be rescued—that I believed I needed a man to provide for me. I would do or sacrifice just about anything to have a relationship.

As I started to recover, I noticed I would have withdrawals in moments of loneliness. I would get an insatiable desire for attention, so I would get dressed and head out to a restaurant, live music, or any place in public where I could get a hit of attention. Like any other addiction, I have learned ways to manage it, but I feel it lingering in the shadows even now. I have had moments of backslide, but I catch them sooner, my recovery time is quicker, and the stronger I recognize my worth, the more distance there is between setbacks.

For years I struggled with my self-esteem, self-confidence, and self-worth. I based my entire life on other people's opinions. Anytime I would have to make a decision, I would ask everyone and anyone their opinion. I trusted the advice of a stranger more than myself. I was constantly giving up my power to others and found myself in a series of unhealthy relationships. Those unhealthy relationships filled every area of my life, from my significant others, bosses, coworkers, friends, and even coaches.

From a very early age, I believed my words didn't matter. While growing up, it didn't feel safe to speak my truth. It often ended up in an argument and then getting the cold shoulder, which for me—a people pleaser—was extreme torture. Being ignored when you believe that the only way someone will love you is when you please them is emotional warfare. After an argument, I would immediately try to please them so they would speak to me. At times, the lengths I went to felt humiliating, but feeling humiliated was far better than the extreme of being thrown out or disowned.

I struggled so much in my teens with finding my voice that the only way I found to express myself was with food. I developed anorexia nervosa. Food was the only thing I felt like I had control over. I would refuse to eat, which led to long nights of battles of the will with my parents. I would sit at the table, refusing to eat until it was bedtime only to wake up the next morning to find dinner was now breakfast. Even if I ate something against my will, I could easily disappear to the nearest bathroom and dispose of it. I would look in the mirror at myself with disgust, and even though I was extremely thin, what I saw was an ugly, overweight version of myself. I wasn't very nice to myself.

Looking back, I wonder if out of all the verbal and emotional abuse I have encountered over the years, was I my own worst offender? Because I used to believe that my self-worth lay with men, I made many bad choices over the years. I did things that, looking back, I want to smack myself for and say *What were you thinking?*

Discovering my voice didn't happen overnight. In fact, it was happening even during the experiences I briefly just touched on. It took my willingness to look at myself—and sometimes not in ways I wanted to see. Through years of self-examination, reading, classes, coaches, and retreats, I found the necessary tools. What is truly beautiful is standing in your power, owning your voice, and speaking your authentic truth. Self-love nourishes the soul and feeds our passion.

As I approached fifty, there was a fork in the road. I could stay in my current relationship and follow my mother's footsteps of being an addict and self-sacrificing for a man or jump without a parachute on a journey of self-exploration and recovery.

If you want to know the juicy details of my latest slip, grab popcorn and read on. I encourage you to learn from my mistakes and how I ended up falling in love with myself and choosing me before anyone else.

LET'S MAKE A DEAL-BREAKER

Just like other times, I regretted my decision to join the dating site within the first twenty-four hours. But there was part of me that longed for attention and connection. I promised myself I would not spend hours or waste energy by mindlessly swiping. I was going to let my suitors come to me. If they reached out, I would review their profiles to see if we had any common interests or if they had any deal-breakers (small children, separated, smokers, heavy drinkers, drugs, etc.). I also paid close attention to what their profile said to determine if I would respond. This was a significant improvement from years prior; I used to feel obligated to respond to everyone.

Most of the men didn't make it past a few text exchanges. If they did make it to the next level, I used the video chat within the app to hide my personal information. If they refused the video chat, that immediately eliminated them. If they passed the video chat, I would exchange phone numbers.

One man caught my attention. We had a lot of common interests: riding motorcycles, traveling, and food. We had a fun video chat, and after I slept on it, I gave him my phone number. We had several phone conversations at first. He made me laugh, and I thought we might even hit it off. Then I noticed that after several phone calls and text exchanges he would go silent. I called him out on this behavior, and he appeared to course correct, so I decided to go out with him.

We agreed to meet at a restaurant on the beach, a short walk from my home. If we enjoyed each other's company and I felt safe, we'd go on a motorcycle ride. I packed my helmet and motorcycle jacket in a backpack and walked downtown to meet him.

As I approached the restaurant, we saw each other and I thought, *Well, hello there, handsome.* Patrick was tall, muscular, and good-looking. He looked even better in person than in his photos and our video chat. With that smile, I knew I would be in trouble. We ordered a few appetizers, and I ordered water. I wanted to be alert and aware, especially if I planned to get on the back of his bike for a ride. He did order a beer, but he only had one, and with his size (over six feet and his muscular body type) and the time we spent talking before we decided to head out, I felt confident and safe. Plus I had a plan B in case things went awry. With my phone fully charged, I had both apps for shared rides downloaded, updated, and ready to use. I had cash on me as well as my credit card and ID. I also took pictures of his profile and phone number and shared them with a friend, who I kept updated on my whereabouts as the date progressed.

I love riding on motorcycles; it is so freeing. I even have my license, but I prefer riding on the back of someone else's bike. Nothing is better than having the wind in my face and taking in all the beautiful nature surrounding us. We decided to drive along the ocean to a more prominent beach town with a hot hangout spot. It was a perfect day for a bike ride! It wasn't too hot or too cold. Along the way, I took in the views of the beaches, ocean, beautiful luxurious homes, and yachts. It felt very comfortable, and being on the back of this gorgeous man's bike, holding on tight, I found myself occasionally caressing his back.

We arrived at our destination and walked through the town. We stopped in a Mexican restaurant for something light to eat and to try a small flight of tequila samples. We had a great conversation. He showed me beautiful pictures of the places he had visited. He had done things on my own bucket list, such as seeing the hot-air balloons take off from Mexico. He had been to Spain and Greece. It seemed as if we had so much in common. Then he started to ask questions about my past relationships. He wanted more details than I was willing to give. I told him that would be a conversation for another time. I noticed that when I asked him questions, he answered them vaguely. Maya Angelo said, "When someone shows you who they are, believe them the first time." He told me he is an open book but keeps things close to his chest. That was the first time I made a mental note.

After the restaurant, we walked through town, and he showed me all the hot spots. While walking through the park, he began to talk about Christmas and something about our children and us all being together. I didn't think much of it, and we moved on to other conversations.

Since our date appeared to be going so well, we left and headed back toward my neighborhood to go to Top Golf to hit some golf balls. On our bike ride back, he made an observation that I (Lorilyn) had been waiting a long time to have fun like this with someone. I threw that same statement back at him and asked, "You haven't?"

We had a blast golfing. We laughed, and Patrick coached my swing. It had been many years since I last played golf. It was a fun night. At some point, he made another comment about my having longed for affection for a long time. This one made me think, huh, and I noted that comment. Yet he wasn't wrong. I had been waiting for someone who was compatible with me. Who loves to ride and have fun, is spontaneous, loves adventure, food, and travel. He also wasn't wrong that I longed for touch. Touch is one of my love languages, but it is also a dangerous one for me. Over the past few years, I had created healthy ways to fulfill my need for touch. I would get regular massages, pedicures, and even go salsa dancing. But being around a man I was physically attracted to was like going to an all-you-can-eat buffet when you are starving.

Before our date, I had promised myself that I would not fall into old behavior. I learned in yoga teacher training that we all have stories called *samskaras*. My teacher explained that our memories are a record in our minds. A record has lines the needle follows to play the song (in our case, our stories). The deeper the groove, the harder it is to jump to the new song. When we re-create our stories, we skip the brain's frontal lobe where discernment lies. If we can "pattern interrupt," we can skip or jump that song on the record, going from our subconscious thoughts that run on autopilot and bringing it into our conscious awareness—where we can then engage our frontal lobe to make new decisions.

After we finished our time at Top Golf, we went to my house so I could change my shoes and shirt for a walk on the beach. He was a gentleman the entire evening. When we got to the beach, he offered to let me sit between his legs and lean my back into his chest like a human lounge chair. Oh my goodness, this was like I had died and gone to heaven. Being held in this man's beautiful muscular arms felt terrific and safe. He talked about his love for the arts, dancing, and travel. We shared stories of the last shows we'd seen. Patrick seemed to align with everything I was looking for in a relationship. Was this guy for real?

We shared our first kiss. His lips were so soft, like pillows. It was slow and sensual; if I hadn't already thought I was in trouble, I knew it for sure at that moment. I could have melted away, but then he made a comment that awakened my frontal lobe like a bad dream. He said, "You are a queen with a kingdom already. You do not need a king; you need a knight—someone who will fight for and protect you."

I thought that his statement was way too smooth. Shortly after that comment, I decided to call it a night while I still had my wits about me. I walked him to his bike. He asked me out again, and I agreed. We made plans to go out the following Sunday after I returned from my business trip, and then he drove off.

The next day, I thought of him more than I wanted to but refrained from texting him. Finally, later that afternoon, he texted me what a wonderful evening he had and how he was looking forward to our date the next Sunday. I responded to him soon after but received no reply. It was several hours before I heard from him again that day. This time I didn't answer until later, and again, silence.

An entire day went by with no response. My stomach was not happy. Oh no. This feeling felt familiar but not in a good way. I was experiencing unexplained feelings of anger. That night, I could not sleep. I was tossing and turning. Finally, at two a.m., I got up and started to journal about my feelings. While out of his sexual energy, I could process by engaging my conscious mind and using my discernment. As I played back the day of our date, I noticed my yellow flags were actually red flags, tainted by temptation.

On what normal date does a guy tell you things like, "I bet you have been longing for physical touch for a long time," or "You have been waiting a long time to have fun with someone." That is not normal; it is called grooming. It is about laying down thoughts so that I would then accept them as my truth. If I did, my mind would say yes, it has been a long time, and then I would accept behavior down the road that wouldn't be acceptable because I now believe I'd waited so long, and here he is!

Did I want to let him go? I had waited to have fun and experience an affectionate touch from someone I found attractive. Did I really want to go back to being lonely?

All the talk about Christmas (which was over nine months away at the time) and bringing our children together is what psychologists call "future faking." A person will tell you something they think you want to hear or experience, knowing that you will never actually ever get it. It is like giving a duck a few breadcrumbs to get them to follow you and never actually giving them enough to sustain them. It works to keep them hungry, so they continue to follow, hoping and wishing you will give them more.

If you find yourself saying, "Is this guy too good to be true?" as I had questioned on my date, the answer is yes! When we go on dating sites or share on social media, we give away a lot of personal information; sometimes people use that information to become the things we seek. I have a small social media presence because of this. I am mindful of what I put out for the public to learn.

I am grateful for his knight comment. It was the pattern interruption I needed to pop my bubble, and it created an opportunity for me to make a new choice. I ended the evening so I could go home and be with my thoughts to get out of my emotions and, if I am honest, my hormonal response.

His texting and then going radio silent is known as "ghosting." It is another grooming tool. It is designed to create a chemical response in the body like a drug. There was a scientific study on cats years ago. They trained the cats to ring the bell, and they would get catnip. Soon the cats were ringing the bell all the time. This is a similar response when we hear the dings of our texts or other notifications. Soon we are like the cats, checking our phones constantly, looking for our next hit.

Because I am aware of these behaviors, I was able to make a new choice. I immediately canceled my dating app membership and deleted my profile. Then I went to his number, blocked him, and then deleted his texts and contact information from my phone. The entire time I was doing this, my ego was fighting me. It wanted me to gather more evidence. It thought we should at least go out one more time to have fun; we deserved it.

But I reminded myself that the last time I went out for "one more time of fun," it had led me to a life-or-death fork in the road, which I will discuss in a later chapter.

This time I chose not to gaslight myself with such lies about needing more evidence or how I deserved to have at least one more fun day. The cost was way too high, and I knew it. Plus my body and intuition were already guiding me, and it was about time to follow that. As a dear friend once said, "I had my own back."

It was time to make new choices and tell new stories where the grooves on the record would be more profound than the old ones. There was and is part of me that is like the cat wanting more catnip and being pissed off that the bell no longer works. Even though I know that one more night could have had costly consequences, it was tough to let it go. The good news is that if I can breathe into it, this too shall pass.

I intend for you to be inspired through my stories and sharing of actionable steps to reconnect with your own authentic voice. You will learn to break the addiction and fall in love with the most important person, you! When you love yourself, everything else falls into alignment. You will be moved to take action and make positive changes in your own life.

Now, I didn't arrive overnight, so to understand how I got here, let's take a little journey.

CHAPTER TWO

GROOMED FROM THE WOMB

I have been powerless around men: I have always placed the needs and desires of men before my own and, embarrassingly, even those of my children. I suspect this might have begun in my mother's womb, as she, too, lived her life trying to please others—especially my dad—even at the risk of her own well-being. My mom was adopted by a woman who made her quit high school when she was sixteen to work full time for a phone company. At the end of the week, my mom would hand over her paycheck to her. In her free time, she cooked and cleaned. She was a living Cinderella. She never finished high school. When she met my dad, my grandmother would try to chase my father away by spraying him with the garden hose. As soon as my mom turned eighteen, she married my dad. It was a small ceremony at the justice of the peace with just two of their friends as their witnesses. My mother worked at the phone company until she got pregnant with her first child, my sister. She went on to give birth to my two brothers, all in three-year increments. I was born nine years later, after my third sibling. I was a twinkle in my dad's eye or, most likely, a midlife-crisis baby.

I grew up on Long Island, New York. We had a typical suburban, male hierarchy "Ward and June Cleaver" family in the 1980s. My parents had old-fashioned values and played the typical roles of married men and women. My dad worked full time as a letter carrier for the United States Postal Service. He would take care of the car, yard, and any projects around the house. My dad also handled all the finances. My mom was a stay-at-home mother and took care of the cooking, cleaning, and the children.

Our family didn't talk about much; dinners were mostly silent. After we finished eating, my dad would get up and most nights go to his basement where he would drink beer and watch TV until he went to bed. My mom would clean up and then spend most of her evenings watching TV in our living room. They didn't communicate or show much affection. I felt like there was always something hidden. It was uncomfortable to have conversations with my parents or siblings, especially around taboo topics like sex, religion, money, personal feelings. I never felt comfortable asking a family member for help. In fact, people would tell me to ask my parents for help, but if I did, it was only when I was desperate. It was emotionally painful to ask for help, and nine out of ten times I was turned away. My parents believed in tough love.

If one of us misbehaved, my mom would threaten us with *Wait until your dad comes home*. There was typical arguing like in most families, but I most hated the cold-shoulder treatment from my mom whenever we had a disagreement. It felt like anytime I didn't agree with her, she would stop talking to me. Talk about mental warfare... to me, the silent treatment was by far the worst. Not being spoken to and trying to fix it to get my fix of verbal communication was the worst punishment I could receive. But my cruelest fear of them all was the simmering fear of being disowned or thrown out. I can remember periods of time when my parents would not talk to one of my siblings for weeks or months at a time due to a disagreement. I was kicked out as a teenager on multiple occasions, usually by my mother when I questioned her authority. My dad never got involved unless my mother requested his assistance if I became too rebellious.

From an early age, I was uncomfortable with speaking up. Then it was further embedded when I was seven years old and was held up at gunpoint in a bank. My mom and I had been out and about running our daily errands. We were making a left turn into the bank parking lot. A gentleman was making a right turn. He of course had the right of way but gestured for us to go first. We parked and walked into the bank, and as my mother was approaching the teller, we heard "Put your hands up, this is a robbery." I can remember my mother turned around and said, "You have to be kidding me." The kind man who waved us in was now wearing women's pantyhose over his head and threatening us with a rifle of some sort. He ordered us all to drop to the floor with our heads down and hands above them. Being only seven and scared, I had an issue with staying still. My whimpering and fidgeting made the robber angry. He kept yelling for me to be quiet and stay still.

I didn't see it myself, but I remember being told a customer came up to the drive-in window and, seeing there was a robbery in progress, left to call the police. Since it was in the late '70s, we didn't have cell phones. I remember watching the robber backing out of the door as I saw his silhouette holding the gun and a bag. Once the police officers arrived, I remember them talking to my mom and the others. It felt like we were there for an eternity. They kept giving me lollipops to soothe me.

That experience stayed with me for many years. I was scared to enter a bank until recently! I can only imagine what that did to my subconscious around money and my voice. And how that robbery many years ago held me hostage for most of my life.

Around the age of ten, I felt like an only child. My sister had married at eighteen, my oldest brother followed her lead and got married at eighteen as well. My closest sibling joined the Navy at seventeen, leaving me, at age eight, home alone during a challenging time for my mother.

As a teenager, I remember my mom crying one day. The women she called her friends had been talking about my mom when she walked in on their conversation. She was devastated. From that point on, she did not spend much time with people outside our home. I believe that had a significant impact on me, especially during my high school years. To this day, I do not feel like I fit into any group. I have always felt like an outsider.

Since I can remember, my mom was always on a fad diet. That part of my childhood had a huge impact on my own self-esteem. I watched my mother struggling on a regular basis with her weight and trying to be perfect. She didn't allow us to have "fattening" snacks in the house. I can remember my dad and I taking a bike ride up to the Carvel ice cream store. We would eat our ice cream on the curb and then ride home.

In hindsight, I can see that my mom suffered from depression throughout my childhood. I remember she attempted suicide on more than one occasion and had a couple of nervous breakdowns. One day I came home from junior high school and found the vacuum had been left in the middle of the floor. I was told that she tried to take her own life. I was devastated. For years, I was angry at her for this because I had not yet matured enough to know she was dealing with a mental illness and probably menopause too. All I knew was that my mom... was not like my friends' moms.

When my mom was in the hospital, I remember having to stay with my sister. I always thought it was a bit weird that I couldn't stay at home. Although I never got a real answer to that, I believe it had to do with my relationship with my dad. Which had its own issues.

In my journey of healing, I have been told by therapists and other professionals that I show signs of having been sexually abused at a young age. While not overt, I do have certain flashbacks from around age three until I reached puberty of me in bed with my dad or him coming into my room, but they are not of him violating me. I know it is hard to hear, but don't worry. Years later, I confronted my dad in one of the most uncomfortable yet powerful conversations I have ever had. I will share that conversation with you in a later chapter. I can remember not being able to sleep some nights because I would wait to hear my father come up the stairs from his den. Until my early forties, I was a light sleeper. I have even slept with a gun under my pillow. Then one day it dawned on me. I was waiting for the sound of footsteps and to hear the click of the light to go on in the hallway.

I know that in my earlier years my dad and I did a lot of things together. He used to take me for bike rides to the park. I always hated it when he would ride ahead and hide. I can remember peddling through on the trail and being scared of every bush and any noise. He would wait until I passed and then sneak up on me and scare me. To this day, I don't like it when people do this.

Sometimes my dad would take me to work with him and I would ride in the back of his mail truck. I don't remember many fun memories with my dad, but going to work with him felt like a treat. He would rack his mail, and I would drink a Mellow Yellow while reading a *Highlight* magazine. The hidden objects activity was my favorite part of the magazine, and I still enjoy them now. I enjoyed my time with my father until one day when I was thirteen it felt like it came to a crashing end. Then, I didn't know why. Looking back, I now realize that was about the time I started my menstruation. Suddenly he stopped taking me to work or taking our bike rides to the park. I felt like I must have done something wrong. I was starving for affection and extremely confused. What did I do to get the cold treatment from my father? I knew I must have done something to cause this. If only I were smarter, prettier, got all A's... the list of my doubts and perceived imperfections goes on and on. I believe it was at that precise moment that I became a perfectionist. If only I could be smart, pretty, skinny, then maybe, just maybe I could get my relationship back with my father.

He became more distant and cold. He only interacted with me during my teens if my mother told him to discipline me. I became angry. My anger often came out with my mother and led us into intense arguments. When I would argue with my mom, I would seek refuge in my bedroom. She would come in and continue to confront me even though I was trying to avoid her. She would back me into the corner. I remember trying to shrink enough to make her go away. If I slammed the door, she would tell me how it was her door and she would remove it. I felt like I had nowhere to hide.

Dinnertime wasn't pleasant for me either. Especially if we were eating something I didn't like. It would become a battle of the wills. I would have to sit at the table until my plate was clean.

I can remember one night having tomato soup for dinner. I despised the aroma and the texture of the vegetables. I ended up sitting at the table until it was my bedtime. The very next morning, guess what was for breakfast?

My mom kept a clean and orderly house. She cleaned the house like it was spring-cleaning every day. She would move the furniture to vacuum, and everything had a place. She expected my clothes to be hung with the same spacing distance in the closet facing the same direction and from light to dark. My drawers also needed to be tidy and everything folded. One day I remember her emptying all my dresser drawers onto the floor in a pile because she thought they were not acceptable. I was supposed to go out with friends, but I no longer could go because I had to fix my room before I could do anything else.

Those arguments sometimes ended up with her throwing my belongings out the window and kicking me out. I was fifteen the first time she told me to get out. One time, I remember being thrown out around Christmas. I was sixteen and my mom only allowed me to take what I had on me. Although I was never in the foster-care system, during my teens I was ultimately taken in by a couple of families in my neighborhood where I found a sense of safety.

As a teen, I had been considered boy crazy, always flirting and seeking male approval. One day in middle school, while proudly wearing a hot new outfit, a boy we called Spider was chasing my friend Karen around. She came to me and asked if she could borrow my belt because her leggings were a bit revealing in the crotch area, and that was why he was running after her. As I began to take my belt off to loan her, he came running after her again. We both started running. I remember approaching the stairwell as a girl said to me,

Why are you running; he is not chasing you! To this day, I can still hear her voice. I took this to heart. It made me feel like I was, like my mom, not enough. This time I was not pretty enough or popular enough.

In the eleventh grade, I knew a lot of people from different cliques, although I never fit in one. I was dating an incredibly handsome and popular soccer player. He was so sweet, and I smile when I think of him. He broke up with me, however, because the girls he hung around with did not like me. I began feeling like I would never be enough for anyone.

Between not feeling like I belonged at school and what was going on at home, I felt like I had no control over my life. As a result, I became anorexic at the age of seventeen. No matter how thin I got, when I looked in the mirror, all I could see was an ugly, overweight girl who was not worthy. I used my anorexia as a way to have a sense of control in my life.

During one of my sessions with a psychologist my mom had gotten for me, I remember asking him, *How do I not become like the members of my family?* I could see that my sister was following my mother's footsteps of depression and breakdowns. His advice was to get out of my home as soon as possible and to continue treatment. I moved into a studio apartment shortly after.

I was a senior in high school when I got my apartment. I was working, so I got out early from school on the work-release program. Moving was just geography. It did not get me away from abusive behavior. I came home from work one day to find that my landlord had gone through my panty drawer. I moved out immediately and found myself back at home once again.

Shortly after my graduation, my parents decided to retire and move to a rural town in North Carolina. It was a very transient town because the military base was less than seven miles away. They invited me to come, but I did not feel the offer was sincere. I could not imagine living under the same circumstances in a whole new environment. I found myself once again homeless.

By the time I was in my twenties, I'd completed the Katherine Gibbs paralegal program. I was working as a legal assistant to an attorney and moonlighting as a cashier and on occasion a cocktail waitress at a night club on the weekends. I was renting the basement apartment from Mr. and Mrs. Magee, neighbors who had at times fostered me. Life was starting to look good.

And then there was the man I let take it all: Vinnie. I wasn't interested in him, but he convinced me to have lunch with him. He pulled out all the stops to woo me. Years later, I learned the correct term: he "love-bombed" me. He sent me dozens of roses, balloons, and chocolates to the law firm. He was from a wealthy family, and we took terrific trips flying first class; his father even closed a restaurant on Long Island to bring our families together for a private Easter celebration. I was head over heels for him, so when he asked me to move in, it was an immediate yes! Fast forward, he broke up with me because he was interested in another woman and I was too nice. According to his friends, he would have probably married me if I hadn't moved in with him. The end of our relationship was the end of my world. I was heartbroken, and my downward spiral began.

CHAPTER THREE

DON'T TAKE MY SUNSHINE AWAY

After the breakup with Vinnie, I was so emotionally distorted that I made poor choices over the next couple of months. I met a bouncer, Frank, at the same nightclub where I'd met Vinnie. At the time, I was desperate for attention, and to be/feel safe again, I agreed to go out with him. He owned a struggling pizzeria and invited me to have dinner with him. Once again, I found myself being love-bombed. It was a private dinner with Frank Sinatra music playing, and we danced in the middle of the restaurant. Before I knew it, we were in bed, and since I struggled with boundaries, I didn't know how at the time to negotiate the conversation around protection. Soon after the first time we had sex, I found myself heartbroken and pregnant at twenty-three. This was one of my most difficult journeys through life. Once I found out I was pregnant, we got engaged to be married, but I noticed concerning behaviors, so I called off the wedding. I decided to take my chances as a single mom. After we separated, I was summoned to court at three month's pregnant to fight for custody of my unborn child because Frank told the judge he was scared I would have an abortion. I had no intention of giving my child up in any form. He wanted custody of our unborn baby from the start.

Pregnant and terrified, I caved and got back together with Frank before our son, Oliver, was born. Only to have him leave me and his mom in the hospital the day we were to take our son home—because I wanted to hyphenate my last name with his on the birth certificate. He pushed the hospital door open so hard it rattled, and he walked out, leaving us sitting there. His mom assured me he would come back, and the nurses asked me if I was safe.

We didn't last much past that. I ultimately had to fight him for custody of my child for years, being dragged through the court system scared, alone, financially and emotionally drained. The irony is that I later surrendered Oliver, at age nine, to him so I could move to Florida with my husband of six years. That decision still impacts me to this day.

It was 1995 when Oliver was born, a time when single mothers were looked down upon in suburban Long Island. It was difficult for me to find a job and an apartment as an unwed mother. The cost of daycare was expensive. I had to work multiple jobs just to make the bills. I tried to get public assistance, but because I worked multiple jobs, I did not qualify for help. I also needed to hire an attorney to maintain custody of my son. Frank was paying the minimum amount in child support because he owned a pizza restaurant that was mostly a cash business and it was difficult to prove what his income was. He also still lived at home with his parents and did not have the same financial obligations as I did. I have no idea why he wanted sole custody of our son; I can only assume it was his ego and he wanted to hurt or punish me for not staying with him.

It was a long, emotionally draining court process that ultimately ended up in the appellate division. That alone cost me thousands of dollars and unquantifiable emotional distress. Frank did not even show up for the hearing, but the appellate court upheld the judge's decision that I have full custody of Oliver.

You would think I would have learned my lesson, but I went on to date several other people and had more unhealthy relationships. I did not realize until many years later that I was re-creating the experience of trying to fulfill the distancing and emotional abandonment by my father.

Like a true addict, I was always looking for my next man fix. I could not go to the grocery store or gatherings without casing the joint and assessing who might be a potential partner. Heck, I even scouted while driving. I tried to please the men in my life by answering their every whim and putting my own needs last. I picked men who spoke poorly to me and validated my story that I was not enough. Each relationship leaned further on the scale of unhealthy.

My last relationship before getting married almost ended my life. I was twenty-seven, a single mother dealing with Frank and his custody court dates when I met Al in 1998. He was a personal trainer at the gym I was going to. He had seven children all by different women and only had custody of his youngest son, Christopher. Al was handsome, charismatic, and as I later learned, a true narcissist. He would say things and then argue he did not say them. It got so bad that I wanted to record our conversations. Even if I had, he would convince me I was wrong. It was an extremely unhealthy relationship that played with my mind and made me feel I was crazy. I still wonder how low my self-esteem was and my need for a man's attention so strong that it allowed a man like Al to manifest in my life.

He was manipulative and chiseled away at whatever self-esteem I had left. One day, I'd had enough. Oliver was at his dad's, and I mustered up the courage to break it off. My friend Laura begged me not to go to his house alone that night. I did not listen to her.

He cornered me in the bathroom and was banging my head against the shower wall while choking me. As I fought, I thought that I would not make it out alive and wondered who would raise my son. I was struggling to stay conscious. I saw a hand mirror out of the corner of my eye. At first try, I could not reach it. By some miracle, I was able to grab the mirror and hit him over the head. It was enough distraction for me to break free and run for the front door, my head and hands bloody from the glass. As I was about to step out of his house, my body was pulled back. He grabbed me by my neck, then threw me into the basement door. Thank goodness it was closed, but the doorknob left a mark on my backside. He then picked me up and flung me over the front stairs and out onto the lawn.

It was at that moment I decided to run. I had enough wits about me to know my car was blocking his car. If he was going to chase me, it would be on foot. I ran into the busy street and down to the corner gas station. I was on the phone with 911, telling them my location, when my cell phone went dead. I remember banging on the window of the gas station, seeing my bloody head in the reflection, begging the attendant to call the police. He refused, saying he didn't want to get involved.

I was terrified that Al would come and find me before the police could when suddenly a young man on a bike appeared from thin air. He assured me I would be okay and he would stay with me until the police arrived. Once the police showed up, he vanished back into thin air. To this day, I still believe he was an angel, the first of many.

The police arrested Al. I had to go to the precinct to file a report. The process was humiliating for me. They took photos of all my injuries, including the impression of the doorknob on my ass. I refused to go to the hospital because it was past midnight and I was tired, scared, and emotionally exhausted.

I finally went home, which was a small room I'd been renting for myself and my son from my best friend's mom, Sally. She was one of the people who would take me in when my mom would kick me out in my teens. The very next night, I overheard Sally telling her boyfriend about my assault the night before. It was almost midnight, and they had been drinking. I confronted her and asked her not to share my personal information with him. She got enraged with my request and began yelling and started to come at me with her fists. Immediately I called my friend, who luckily lived a few houses down the block. She came over to find her mother had me cornered in (yet another) bathroom and was hitting me on the head with the house phone. Once again reinforcing the pattern from my early years that I was not allowed to speak my truth or to set boundaries.

Sally threw us out. At first she would not even let me take our belongings. I was once again homeless, this time with my two-and-half-year-old son. It was a lot to handle all at once. Looking for a new home, managing my emotions from not just one but two physical attacks within twenty-four hours. And the possibility of losing my closest friend, who knew all my childhood secrets. My best friend and I ultimately, thankfully, remained friends after that event only because she had gotten there in time to witness it for herself.

My best friend was a big support to me during my childhood, and again as I pressed charges against my violent, narcissistic ex-boyfriend. Turns out that Al was dishonorably discharged from the services and I was not the first woman he had laid hands on. I went to every court appearance, juggling jobs and day care, to make sure that he could never do this again to anyone. He would blow me kisses across the courtroom in hopes of intimidating me. He and his attorney attempted to get into the same elevator I was in although I had a protection order. His attorney told me to calm down, once again trying to silence my voice. I said, "No, I have an order, and he cannot be in here." They got off that elevator, but later in the parking lot, Al tried to hit me with his car. He would also cross within the legal distance, then slowly drive past to harass me.

The court kept postponing the court dates at every appearance. Almost a year passed, and I had used up every sick and vacation day I had, going to the hearings. Being a single mom and still fending off the court appearances from my son's father, Frank, was heavily tapping my funds, so when the criminal court rescheduled again, I had no choice but to not go to the next date. The district attorney prosecuting Al assured me that nothing would happen and it would be okay for me not to go that one time.

After that next court date, I got a call from the district attorney. She had settled in my absence. They had slapped Al on the wrist and given him probation. The wind was taken out of my chest, and the whole world went into slow motion. Once again, my voice had been robbed. I was angry and extremely upset as I fell to the floor, sobbing. I felt betrayed, my heart hurt, and I gave up on ever having my voice heard and feeling like justice had been served.

With both court cases between Al and Frank coexisting, I was in need of a girl's night out. On a weekend when my son was three years old and visiting his father, I went out dancing with my best friend. At that time, I got lots of male attention: as a side hustle I was a physical trainer and had the body to prove it. I also had a short haircut that had people telling me I looked like Jamie Lee Curtis. While walking through a nightclub that night, a guy grabbed me and said, "I know you." My salty best friend said, "Yeah, we know she looks like Jamie." He said no and called me by my name. Turns out Anthony and I had gone to high school together. He was a year behind me. Flattered by his comments, we closed the club that night dancing.

I was once again swept off my feet, and soon an evening picnic at the beach led me to getting pregnant again. This time I was not going to have a repeat of the last experience, so we agreed to get married.

So in August of 1999, right before my twenty-eighth birthday, I was married, pregnant, and still fighting with Oliver's father over custody. My new husband was very supportive during the process. Johnny was born in 2000, and we rented from Anthony's mom until we purchased our first home in February 2002. We had what most would consider a typical marriage and family life, but we struggled as a couple because we didn't get married for exactly all the right reasons. It was also during that time I met my dear friend Leianne and my first coach who introduced me to self-growth and spirituality. I remember reading Eckhart Tolle's book *The Power of Now*. I was hooked! I wanted to learn everything I could and deep dived into self-study.

Anthony was a union carpenter who worked in Manhattan. When there was work, life was good; when there wasn't, especially after 9/11, we had financial challenges that added to our already struggling relationship. His grandfather had moved to Central Florida and so had his mom and stepdad. With the construction industry booming in Florida, we relocated to Florida in August 2005. With my rose-tinted glasses once again, I had hoped that steady work and geography would save our marriage. But I had to pay the ultimate price. After years of battling with my firstborn child's father and finally being awarded official court custody of Oliver, I gave custody to his father because Frank was not going to let us move out of New York without another custody battle. People started telling me that Oliver would miss me and that he would come home to me in Florida within a year.

Every time I wanted a visit with Oliver, I would have to fly to New York, pick him up, and fly back with him to Florida. I also had to do the same to return him to New York. It was emotionally and financially draining, and if that wasn't enough, the construction industry in Florida began to slow down. I was struggling with having one child in New York and one in Florida. People judged me for leaving my son, but trust me, no one could kick the shit out of me more than I did myself. I had earned a black belt for beating myself up. Not only did all the challenges in my marriage before we moved to Florida return, but I was on the verge of a mental breakdown as the one-year anniversary of leaving Oliver in New York was approaching, and he was no closer to coming home to me.

Once that year hit, it was all downhill for me emotionally even though I was continuing my self-discovery by seeing a therapist and taking several self-help classes from the Landmark Forum. I did not feel like I fit into the area where we lived, our marriage was struggling, I had started my own business as an aesthetician, and we had money issues, which made it challenging to fly round trips to pick Oliver up for visitations.

Locally there had been a surge in teen pregnancies, and because of my experience as an unwed mother, I wanted to support and empower young women. I thought it would be a win-win and give me something positive to focus on. As a result of my own early journey to reclaiming my power, I developed Girlz to Women, a nonprofit organization. Girlz to Women focused on young women leaving elementary school and heading to junior high, which is known as the most vulnerable time for teenage girls. We also focused on using successful high school young women as mentors to the junior high students. Groups were mentored by successful women from the community. Some of the young women participants would come in as juniors and then become successful women mentors. Girlz to Women was featured in several national magazines, but unfortunately, my marriage was falling apart and I could not keep it going any longer. I went into a deep depression, and ultimately my marriage ended amicably with shared custody of Johnny.

AFTER A FEW YEARS OF WORKING ON MYSELF—I SUPPORTED A HOST OF therapists, coaches, and attended every self-help event available—and being a part-time mom, I thought I was ready to date again. I signed up for an online dating service and met Bob. He was a good-looking Italian from New York. He felt safe and familiar because we had both come from Long Island. And I know what you're thinking: Hadn't I learned anything from my history with Italian men? Very early, the relationship was toxic. My friends saw it, but I wasn't open to hearing it; I was in love! He convinced me to move in with him so I could save money, which was my top priority, and see Oliver and provide for Johnny during the weeks he was with me. But—and this is big—he wanted me to give up my fur baby girl. When I first moved to Florida, my ex-husband, Anthony, had gotten a beautiful Bichon puppy for me. I named her Missy Girl. She kept me company, provided unconditional love, and comforted me during some very hard times. She did everything with me. After my divorce, I went to work for the state attorney's office to have a steady salary and health benefits. But Missy was not used to being home alone and would cry and scratch the apartment door while I was gone. Bob used that to tell me it wasn't fair to her and that his lease did not allow dogs. So not only did I give up my apartment but I gave up my beloved Missy Girl. Once again, I gave up something I loved for a man. Over the next six months, the relationship got more and more toxic. He would tell me things like, I'd better watch myself or he would dump me in the Ocala Forest and no one would ever find me.

My friends—who had tried to warn me in the beginning about my relationship—staged an intervention with me. Their intentions to help me backfired. I ended up denying what they were saying, and as they were tired of watching someone they loved be in an abusive relationship, they ended our friendship. Unfortunately, this isn't uncommon in abusive relationships. The abuser wants to isolate their victim from their friends and family so they will become dependent on their abusers. This intervention played right into the wedge between my friends that Bob was already creating.

Without having the support of friends now, I was right where he wanted me to be—utterly dependent on him. I started to seek a way out when my son, Johnny, told me he didn't like living with Bob. I had a friend named Jen who would secretly meet Johnny and me to look at apartments. If it weren't for her help and support, I would have ended up in a crappy apartment. She convinced me I was worth more and helped us get into a nice, safe apartment complex with a pool and amenities. I had planned to tell Bob about us moving out on a weekend when Johnny was visiting his dad, to keep him safe. But on a Thursday evening in February of 2016, Bob, Johnny, and I were eating dinner when Bob put me on the spot. He had found out I planned to move out that Saturday. It was like walking on eggshells, but I did everything possible to keep the peace until Johnny left for school Friday morning. The following twenty-four hours were some of my scariest moments. I stayed in Johnny's room that Friday night. Notice I didn't say that I slept? Bob would randomly open the door and come into the room. He even walked into the bathroom while I was in the shower to intimidate me and let me know who was in charge. It was a long night. The following day, he left the apartment, willing to allow my friend Jen and a few others to help me move out. We were out in under a few hours. I had my freedom, but I looked over my shoulder for many years after.

CHAPTER FOUR

AN UNCOMFORTABLE CONVERSATION

Fast forward a few years: my years of therapy, classes, and working on myself were coming to fruition. I had become a wellness coach and was a program director of a wellness center and in a relationship with a man who was not abusive but also did not have as much drive as I did. Oliver was still living in New York with his dad, and we would visit on occasion. Since I had been thrown out of my home in my teen years, it was essential to own my own home. That dream became a reality in 2017 when I purchased my town-home. I loved my three bedrooms, two baths, and fabulous screened porch with a view of a most spectacular oak tree that housed many birds who serenaded me in the morning as I drank my coffee. It was in Johnny's school district and made coparenting easy. I loved owning my own home! I thought no one could ever throw me out again. It was extremely empowering.

I was restarting my consultant business. This was when I was first introduced to Human Design by my second coach, Colleen. Human Design is based on six spiritual practices. It uses your date, time, and place of birth to determine your chart. Your chart is like discovering your own unique owner's manual. I mentioned in my Soapbox that this is based on the premise that your soul created your contract before you came into the world. Human Design and understanding my own uniqueness were a huge part of my recovery and why I now use it with all my clients. I will share more in later chapters. Since I was now a homeowner, I felt tremendous responsibility for paying a mortgage and all the other expenses associated with home-ownership.

It was August 2017 when I received a call that my dad was in the hospital and needed surgery. He had a hernia that was wrapped around his testicle, and because of that, his body was backed up with toxins. They had to wait to do the surgery because he was on blood thinners.

Anytime my parents had health issues, I was most often the one to drop everything and go to North Carolina to assist them. It was close to my birthday, and my elementary school best friend was scheduled to come from New York to celebrate with me. I remember quickly packing and getting on the road for the thirteen-hour car ride from Florida to North Carolina. It was an emotional roller-coaster ride as I drove. I experienced all the emotions: fear of losing my dad, anger for having to drop everything to help my parents, especially when I had a visitor coming to town, and every emotion in between.

I was crying hysterically when my phone rang. It was my dear friend and colleague, Connie. I remember contemplating whether I would answer her call, but something made me pick up the call. I yelled out to her, "Connie, you caught me at a bad time." I had to explain to her that I was driving to North Carolina because my dad was facing a life-threatening surgery. Connie immediately put her coaching hat on. See, we were not just friends but also both speakers and trainers. Connie and I had each experienced trauma in our lives.

Connie works with victims of childhood sexual trauma, exploitation, pornography, human sex trafficking, and domestic violence, so when she heard what I was experiencing, she first tried to calm me down. She then went on to say that I should consider confronting my dad about my childhood experiences. I told her I did not feel that was appropriate given the circumstances of him facing a life-threatening situation. That was when Connie said that it is easier to do it on this side of the earth plane than if he should pass over. I understood what she was saying; she was telling me to make peace with him now, or I might regret it for the rest of my life.

Once I understood the potential consequences of not speaking up, Connie began to coach me on what to say. She told me to tell my dad, "We have had some good times and bad times. I know you know what I am talking about. I want you to know that I forgive you, but more importantly, I forgive myself." I contemplated my conversation with Connie for the rest of my car ride to North Carolina. I envisioned what it would be like to have that conversation with my dad. I felt selfish for even considering trying to speak with him while he was facing a life-threatening health crisis. I asked myself if I could follow through with it. After all, I was used to putting other people's needs in front of my own.

After a long and emotional journey, I arrived at the hospital. I remember walking into my dad's hospital room. He looked like the Michelin Tire Man. He looked awful—he was swollen all over his body. I sat in the corner of the room, staring at my dad and repeatedly hearing Connie's words, "It is easier to heal on this side of the plane." I finally mustered up the courage and walked over to the side of my father's hospital bed. With a deep breath, I gently grabbed his hand and said, "Dad, we have had some good times and some not-good times. I know you know what I mean. I forgive you, but more importantly, I forgive myself." I was shocked that I said it, but he did not respond.

I stood there and felt like my entire life was flashing through my mind. I asked myself if I could repeat it. Did I want to repeat it? Was I being completely selfish right now? I heard Connie's voice again. At that moment, I repeated what Connie had coached me to say again, only this time, my father squeezed my hand. I took that as an acknowledgment and felt immediate relief, as if I had been heard for the first time by my father.

My father survived that surgery, and I got to take him home from the hospital. It was a Thursday. I was very hopeful that we had turned a new corner, but as soon as we got to the driveway, my father and his pride refused to follow the hospital discharge orders, and he would not use a walker or a cane to get from the car to the house. He had too much pride to be seen using something like that in public. Once we got into the house, my father immediately opened a can of beer, which was also against the doctor's recommendations.

My father was being ornery, and I disliked how he spoke or behaved toward me. My feelings of hope and healing for our relationship quickly dissipated. I remember being in the kitchen with my mom, telling her that I didn't have to put up with such behavior. I was no longer five and would not hide in a corner; after all, I was a grown woman who owned a home and a business.

I left for the pharmacy to pick up my dad's prescriptions, then called my coach, Colleen, and told her about everything that was happening. She said that I did not have to stay there and care for my parents. Leaving them went against every fiber of my being, but I was no longer willing to sacrifice my well-being. I called my brother to explain I was done, and he agreed to come to North Carolina and take over. When I returned from the stores, I let my mother know I would leave on Saturday morning and that my brother would arrive sometime Saturday afternoon.

My dad asked me to sit with him the next day, Friday. He said, "I don't know why I behaved the way I did, but I am sorry." I was in shock! I had never heard my dad say he was sorry. I took that as a huge win. I did leave the following day as planned, but what happened after that was truly life-changing.

Before my conversations of forgiveness with my dad, in the hospital and after he returned home, whenever I would call my parents, my dad would answer the phone and quickly hand me off to my mom without even saying a word. After we spoke, he sounded like a kid in an ice cream shop when I called. We would talk for long periods of time. When I visited him for his eightieth birthday in September 2019, he was on the front porch, eagerly awaiting my arrival. We immediately went to the back porch and talked for hours.

I remember us going to the store and laughing and joking. He bought me a portable speaker that day, which I still have and protect as if it were a national treasurer. Finally it was the relationship I had been longing for with my father almost my whole life.

As uncomfortable as the hospital discussion with my dad was, it was one of the most life-changing moments I have had. See, that talk with my dad did not just free me; it freed my dad too. It allowed us to finally have a relationship. From that moment forward, I committed to learning how to be comfortable with having uncomfortable conversations. Sometimes I get caught up in my fear, and I remind myself that if I could confront my dad, I can have just about *any* uncomfortable conversation.

After seeing the change that happened with my dad, I decided to embrace uncomfortable situations in every area of my life. I first sat down with my sons and told them I was sorry for some of the choices I had made and for any impacts they might have had on them. I explained to them that I now understand why I had behaved in the ways I did. I shared that I thought I needed a man to take care of us, so I had made decisions that were not always in our best interests. I asked them if they had any anger, questions, or issues with me that they would like to discuss. My sons' responses to our uncomfortable heart-to-heart were filled with understanding and showed me tremendous grace. At that time, neither of them had any situations that needed to be addressed. They both told me that they understood that I had made what I thought were the best choices at that time and that they are now both grown men who are responsible for their life choices.

I told them my regrets of not having had that discussion with my dad sooner, to have embraced a genuine connection sooner, and I did not want to wait until I was on my deathbed to have them with my children. I wanted to own anything I had done and give as much closure as possible to my sons. I promised that moving forward, they would always come before my other relationships, and I would speak to them *first* before anyone else, especially when making life choices that could impact them. Like this book you are reading.

I also use this as an example when I am coaching clients. I tell them the more uncomfortable they are, the more excited I get. They often look at me like I am crazy after I say that. I then tell them the good news: the more uncomfortable they are, the bigger the reward. See, my only regret was that my dad passed away soon after his eight-ieth birthday, after we had that uncomfortable conversation. I wish I'd had more time with him. I often wonder what would have happened if I'd had that conversation sooner. It taught me that life is too short to wait to speak my truth to avoid being uncomfortable. The cost is too high.

CHAPTER FIVE

THE LOUDEST VOICE

After confronting my dad and finally having the relationship with him I had desired my entire life, things looked to be going well for me in 2018. My speaking and consulting business was growing, and I loved owning my own home. I was starting to feel like my life was finally heading in the right direction.

I enjoyed traveling and delivering keynote presentations and workshops at conferences across the United States, as well as consulting and training organizations in the communication methodology I created called CHAT. Nothing makes me feel more aligned with my purpose than when I am standing on a stage or supporting someone to be their authentic self. Johnny was eighteen and decided to live with his dad full time. I didn't love his choice, but I honored his feelings and desires; after all, he was now of legal age to make those choices. My home felt empty at times, but it was my sanctuary, especially my screened-in porch with the view of an amazing old oak tree that gave me inspiration when thinking about how many storms it had made it through. And that it was still standing.

Because I always felt like I needed more credentials, I had completed a certification course at a local speakers academy (which was where I had met my dear friend Connie, who'd helped me with the tough conversation with my dad). I then joined an association of speakers from all over the country as a professional member because I thought I needed to learn even more and wanted to network with other professionals who had more speaking experience.

I attended regular meetings, volunteered, and even went on to be the associate dean of the academy I had attended. There was a member named Richard who would pop up at meetings every once in a while. He was always nice to me when I saw him, was very charismatic, and everyone spoke highly of him.

There was much networking and sharing within the group, and I believe most people participated from a kind heart. Like Brady, who introduced me to his contact who selected speakers for an international professional association. I was later asked to present at their annual conference. I was beyond excited to be invited to speak to an audience full of people who had the potential to hire me for their clients' conferences. It was a big moment, and I was excited about the opportunity.

The conference was held in Indiana. I arrived in Indianapolis on a Saturday in early June. I wanted to be part of the entire conference to network and observe other speakers. My session was being held on Monday. Shortly after arriving, I received a Facebook message from Richard. He saw that I was in Indiana, and he happened to be there as well, not for the conference but for a client of his. He invited me to have dinner with him on Sunday evening. I asked him for a different night as I had my big day on Monday, but he was leaving town, so I agreed. I told him I didn't want to be out too late.

I met Richard at one of the most expensive steakhouses I have ever visited, where we consumed exceptional food and beverages. Afterward, he offered to show me around town, and I said yes, as long as I wasn't out too late. The next thing I knew, we were inside a Cinderella-shaped horse and buggy and riding around a quaint downtown area. After the tour, he wanted to show me his favorite place: an upscale cigar bar. We were chatting on a couch when Richard mentioned something about his wife. I was caught off guard. I never knew or had an inkling he was married. He had never spoken of his wife before and didn't wear a wedding band. He saw I was shocked. I told him I thought he was single. He laughed and said, "No, I am not single," and then said, "Oh my goodness, I took you on a fairy-tale horse and buggy ride. That must have been confusing."

Yeah, you think, Richard? Of *course* I thought he was trying to woo me, and I was always on the lookout for a potential mate. I felt stupid and tremendously embarrassed. I left shortly after that conversation, as I could not let it get to me. After all, I was already worried that my nerves would keep me up all night, and I wanted to be well rested and give it my all for my talk the next day.

I gave a great presentation called Let's CHAT, based on my communication system. In fact, my room was filled, and people stood in the back and out into the hallway. In the end, people waited in line for over an hour to speak with me. I was sure this would be the beginning of a new level of my success! Richard called me later that day to see how I made out. I thought that was genuinely nice of him.

Back in Florida, he and I communicated over the next several days. Richard was a successful speaker with impressive credentials after his name. He offered to help me with my speaking business, but during a few of our conversations, he made a number of offensive or inappropriate comments, which I confided to another female colleague and friend, Sherri. Sherri was tall and gorgeous and had been a model in her younger years and still dressed to turn heads. Sherri was someone I quickly became close to. She showed me how to live in style! I treasured our time together, but I realize now that we bonded so quickly because we "trauma bonded." Trauma bonding is when hurt people immediately share their wounds from a wounded place. It can feel like an instant connection and closeness, but it can be very toxic as both people are still working through their traumas.

Richard's story then changed from our earlier conversation at the conference. He confessed that he and his wife were still married but that he was living in the guest house above the garage. That update didn't change the way I felt about him. He was married, and I wanted just to have a professional relationship.

I had shared with Sherri some of the inappropriate comments Richard had made and how I wanted to limit my communication with him. She told me that a man with desires—and who had influence—could be a powerful ally. Being in the modeling industry, Sherri knew how to play the games to get what she wanted. Since I believed I needed a man to succeed, I agreed to try to play the game and to create boundaries with Richard.

When Richard asked me to show him around my neighborhood for the Fourth of July weekend, I clearly stated my boundaries. I told him I had no interest in having any kind of romantic or intimate relations with a married man, but we could be friends and colleagues. It was raining, so we rearranged our plans: he brought over all the ingredients to make his favorite cocktail for us. After we'd each had a drink, we took an Uber to a fancy restaurant downtown where we ate and drank like royalty. We then went to my favorite wine bar that friends of mine owned, to dance and listen to music. I had a great time, and Richard was being respectful of my boundaries. I trusted him.

So when I went to the bathroom and then danced with friends, I never thought twice about leaving my drink with him at the table. Richard asked me to dance a little later, and all I remember was that my ankle was rolling underneath me and everything seemed in slow motion. I remember confessing to an influential couple in my community, where I networked and worked, that I thought their adult son was handsome. Oh my goodness, what was I doing? I knew on some level that I was making an ass out of myself. The next thing I remember is getting out of an Uber at my house. I don't even remember getting into the Uber.

I will tell you that this is where the story gets emotionally difficult for me to write. It was like someone randomly turned my lights on and off, from being conscious to unconscious. I don't remember walking to or from the Uber, and I have no idea how we got into my home. The next thing I remember is sitting on my couch in my living room with Richard sitting across from me—when all of a sudden his hand was up my shorts and touching my genitals. I remember asking him what the hell he thought he was doing, and then it went black.

When I came to, I was lying on my bed, and I saw Richard walking down my hallway, naked. I could not move, and I wasn't awake for more than a few seconds. Later that evening, I was woken up by Richard banging and shouting at my door. I have no idea how I got up and made it to the door to let him in, and I don't remember anything after that. I can only assume that he had left something important in my home and realized it after he let himself out.

When I finally woke up, it was only then I realized I was naked and in my bed and had no idea how or why. I have no idea how many hours I was blacked out—and have no idea what time it was when I did black out—and I can't remember when I was finally able to get out of bed. If I had to guess, it was around seven p.m. the day after. When I did get up, I felt like I was drunk. I could hardly walk. I thought, Wow, those drinks had to be strong; I have never been this drunk. I remember googling how to cure a hangover. I could not even make myself food. I shook from standing. I contemplated taking myself to the emergency room, but I could not walk straight, nevertheless drive. I was too embarrassed to call a friend; I couldn't remember anything but those few key moments. I went back to bed, and that was when I noticed that my bed was completely off the box spring. Between being naked, sore, and my bed having been moved, I could only assume I had sex with Richard. I had no recollection of it.

The next day, Richard called me to see how I was doing. He offered to come over and bring me breakfast. I agreed to let him come over because I was confused and had no idea what happened. I wanted to confront him to find out. When Richard arrived and I told him how sick I was, he acted shocked. I asked him if we'd had sex, and he said yes, but if he'd had any idea that I was that drunk, he would never have allowed us to.

I was already embarrassed and ashamed and now felt even more so. I wanted to crawl up into a dark corner and disappear. What I didn't catch in the moment because I was too busy shaming myself, was that he went on to say how, when I was lying on the edge of the bed and he needed to get up, *he had pushed me off the bed to get me out of his way.* He then stood up and imitated me. His hands flailed in the air, and he swayed from side-to-side stumbling around, all while making noises. And he was laughing at me. In hindsight, I realize that he did know exactly how intoxicated I'd been; he had just demonstrated that.

After breakfast, which did help my hangover, he suddenly had an interest in helping me with my business. He had always promised to help me in the weeks before but had never followed through. This is common to "bread-crumbing"—dropping little pieces of information that an abusive person knows you want but never actually giving you anything of substance. Think about dropping pieces of bread for ducks and how they will follow you, wanting more. Richard had the bread, and I was the duck following him around thinking he would save me by telling me an industry secret or introducing me to the right connections to have increased success with my business. He had no intention of ever helping me. That day Richard watched my first TEDx talk and gave me feedback. But the feedback he provided only touched the surface and didn't feel sincere. I feel he only pretended to want to help because of the circumstances and his actions. He wanted to give me a bigger breadcrumb to distract me from his motive. And like an addict, I took it because I was eager to make it as a speaker and embarrassed by my behavior. There was nothing in what he shared that would help me build my speaking business or become a better speaker. Before leaving, he reiterated that he had no idea how drunk I had been. I felt awful about myself. How did I allow myself to get so drunk and, even worse, to sleep with a married man? Why didn't I remember anything? I was so embarrassed, and I didn't tell anyone.

Our local speakers association chapter was having a social get-together in Orlando later in July. I was planning on attending, but my car had issues. When one of my fellow members, along with another student in the academy, Tom, found out, they offered to come and pick me up to take me to the event. We had dinner, and afterward,

Richard invited us to join him for a drink at another location. I told Richard that I could not go. But Richard was Tom's mentor, and Richard convinced us to go and have a drink. Once again, feeling safe with my peers, I used the restroom. After one drink, I felt an effect similar to the last time I had a drink with Richard. I said to myself, Wow, I can't hang with him, he drinks some strong shit. Richard offered to take me home for Tom, but Tom refused and said he'd gotten me there and would get me home. On the way home, I don't remember much, but I do remember telling Tom something sexual about myself and purring like a kitten. *Oh my GOD!*

I don't know how I got into my house that night, but I am glad Tom got me home safely. I do remember that in the middle of the night, I answered my phone, and it was Richard asking me to do something sexual, but I was once again so out of it that I blacked out. This time the recovery was not as long but still not normal for a hangover.

I kicked the living shit out of myself over it. I ran both evenings repeatedly in my mind. I called myself awful things. My self-esteem was so low—and having been groomed to please men—that when Richard asked me to meet him at a hotel a couple of weeks later, I did. True to being an addict, I somehow justified that I wanted to do this because I had already crossed those lines with him the night I can't remember, and he was supposedly separated from his wife. I can't really understand now, even years later, why I went. He brought coffee, and I wanted to drink coffee and have a conversation, but he was eager to get straight to sex. I didn't realize he was dressed in gym clothes with a gym bag, but I now realize that he must have told his wife he was going to the gym. Richard was in a rush to get to it, but he was unable to perform and became angry. He left cash on the nightstand to pay for the hotel room and left. I felt dirty and gross. I felt like I had sold my body—and didn't even get paid or receive the emotional fix I wanted. I was even more confused and felt myself slowly shutting down.

I started avoiding friends and stayed home alone. I had no drive to work. At our professional convention, I was so paranoid that any male who looked at me triggered me. Over the next several weeks, Sherri and a few others noticed my odd behavior. I denied it and then started avoiding them, also typical behavior of an addict.

At that time, during every free second of my life, I analyzed the first evening I blacked out. It literally was any free minute. I was obsessed with it. I could not sleep or work. The scenario played in my head over and over again like a broken record. I could not think of anything else. I shamed and blamed myself constantly. My ego had a field day with every thought about what an idiot I was.

My dear friend Tracey was one of the first friends I'd made when I moved to Florida, and she was having her ribbon cutting for her new massage office in early August. I was honored to help her run the event, and since I didn't want anyone to know of my bad choices, I was able to find the focus to do so.

The day of Tracey's event I went to the bank, and while I was waiting in line at the drive-through, I got an idea to google alcohol poisoning. Although some of the symptoms matched what I had experienced, it didn't explain some of the other symptoms. Moments later, I was inspired to google "being roofied." The moment I started to read the symptoms, they matched my experience to a tee. I broke down sobbing in my car while waiting for the teller.

I knew I had to pull myself together for Tracey's ribbon cutting, which I somehow did. I can only assume that my previous life experiences had taught me how to shove my feelings so far down so I couldn't feel them. I had learned how to become numb to survive. I have no idea how I made it through that event, but later that evening, I had a breakdown. It was the first time I seriously contemplated taking my own life. I was in a very dark place emotionally. I had been holding in all my emotions for over a month. Once again, my phone was ringing at the right moment, and although I did not want to pick it up, something made me. It was my friend Sherri. Like Connie who'd called when I was spiraling out of control driving to North Carolina for my dad, Sherri was also a trained professional coach and immediately recognized I was suicidal. Sherri said something that pissed me off. She had done it on purpose. On the scale of emotions, depression is one of the lowest, with love being the highest. Sherri had known that to keep me safe, she needed to get me higher on the scale, and anger was above depression.

When I told Sherri everything that had happened, all my odd behavior over the past month made sense to her. She felt hurt that I didn't feel safe enough to share this with her earlier, but I felt guilt and shame *and blamed myself* for my behavior. How could I tell anyone? When I'd found out that I was drugged by someone I had trusted and respected, I played back our conversations—of Richard making fun of me, telling me he had no idea how drunk I was, that he wouldn't have touched me if he'd known—I was filled with rage. Not only did he drug me and rape me, but he then belittled and blamed me. Holy shit, I was losing my mind as all those thoughts swirled in my head. The only way I thought I could get out of the pain in that moment was to take my own life.

Sherri was pulled over on the side of the road, on the phone, fighting for my life. She finally got me to a safe headspace and— knowing that integrity is my number one value—made me promise to call and get help.

The next day, I called the women's shelter and made an appointment for the Rape Crisis Center. My next tough and humiliating call was to my dear friend Karen, whom I had met several years prior at a Unity church. We loved being roommates at conferences and had wonderful soulful conversations. Of course, we also giggled like little girls at times. Because Karen made me feel safe and was very compassionate—and I knew she would not judge me—she was the person I asked for help. I briefly cried through telling her what had happened and asked her if she would be willing to take me to my appointment.

When Karen picked me up, she exuded caring and allowed us to drive in the uncomfortable silence. It was a humbling experience for me when we arrived at the shelter. See, I had formerly gone to this shelter and shared my stories of abuse with domestic violence survivors as inspiration for them to keep moving forward beyond their experiences. And here I was about to go in, not as a guest speaker but as a victim. I silently read the sign above the door, RAPE CRISIS CENTER, and I was once again paralyzed. But not from drugs, this time with fear, guilt, and shame.

Karen came inside and supported me as I completed my paper-work and sat in the waiting room when I went to see the therapist. As I shared what I remembered with my counselor, she confirmed that I was most likely drugged, from all the side effects I'd had. She was concerned that I could have overdosed because of how long my side effects lasted and told me how I was lucky to have survived. There was no physical evidence since I hadn't gone to the emergency room. I wished I had followed my intuition to get help the day after the attack, but I hadn't. And now, if I wanted to press charges, it would be Richard's word against mine. We all know how those cases publicly play out in our society: the victim is usually prosecuted instead of the perpetrator.

I was later told by some of my female colleagues that I would be committing professional suicide if I decided to press charges—but I had almost taken my own life trying to hide what had happened! I was even told that Richard's behavior displayed sociopathic or psychopathic tendencies and that if I wanted to prosecute him, I could put myself in harm's way, because people who have personality disorders lack emotions and care more about protecting their assets and reputation than other human beings. Terrified and full of shame, I didn't file charges. I suffered alone even though I was seeing the therapist from the rape center regularly.

Once I figured out that Richard had drugged me, I never spoke to him again. I was terrified to go to our association meetings, fearing that he would be there, but I had made professional commitments and didn't want to tell anyone else what had happened. Every time I would have to go to a meeting, I went to great lengths to determine if Richard would be there. I think my sudden silence scared him away from attending meetings. I am sure I wasn't the first person he had done this to, and in my mind, I justified why he would randomly show up and then disappear. My friend Sherri said she would have my back if he ever did show up. She told me not to let him "shrink me" anymore by dropping out of our association. I will always be grateful to Sherri for saving my life.

My depression continued to grow. I was a professional speaker whose voice was once again silenced. Until I decided I wanted to take my power back. Since it was too late to press charges against Richard, as months passed, I needed to find a way for me to get my power back both personally and professionally. Not speaking my truth, staying silent, was fueling my depression and I felt like my soul was dying because I was not living with purpose. I had to do something, so I reached out to the president of the national association to present an idea I had.

The national association president agreed to meet with me. He is a Christian man whom I respected, especially because his wife had her own survival story. I figured if anyone would understand me, it would be this man. I didn't just want to go to the meeting with a problem, I wanted to be part of the solution. I researched and created a plan and an outline for a new committee called Stand by You. The idea behind the committee would be to support victims—whether it was an association member who took advantage of them, from selling them bad products to drugging and raping them, and anything in between. The committee members would walk the victim through the proper processes to file complaints within the association's rules and guidelines.

At my meeting, I started by sharing my story without naming Richard. I was amazed when the president then told me that at the conference that same year, another female member had been drugged, but luckily, she made it back to her room by herself before she was assaulted. Clearly there was a problem that needed to be addressed in the association. I explained that I believed the association was a perfect ecosystem for predators.

I shared that I also believe that many speakers have some attributes of narcissism. Victims often want to become speakers to share their survival stories to help other potential victims from having the same fate. Narcissists feed off victims, and victims often feel drawn to help change narcissists. It is a never-ending unhealthy cycle.

At the end of our meeting, the president told me he would convey my ideas to the association, but I never heard anything from him after our meeting. It was suggested that I bring my committee idea to our local chapter to present Stand by You at one of our regular meetings. I was supported by Connie and a few other members who helped pitch the idea to the membership during our monthly gathering.

I remember standing at the front of the room, delivering the concept. I felt empowered, but it didn't last long. My proposal made it to the board agenda only to be buried. Once again, I found myself silenced. At that moment, I decided to end my investment of time, money, and literally my soul, with an association unwilling to create social change.

After the assault, I would have nightmares that Richard would come back and shoot me through the windows. I could not sleep or deal with all my emotions from the assault. The fear, shame, and depression were so debilitating that I could not work, and supporting myself became a challenge. I tried to create solutions to keep my home. I even considered renting it out, getting a roommate, etc. I didn't want to be kicked out and homeless again. I ended up selling my townhome, making enough profit to pay off all my debts. My sons were both over eighteen, independent, and I moved to Tampa because it was a city I was drawn to. I thought being in a new area would make me feel safe.

I had always let other people's opinions and my very loud ego (telling me how I needed a man to make it) drown out my intuition, completely ignoring my inner voice. In Eric Butterworth's book, *Spiritual Economics*, he tells the reader to "Stand guard at the door of your mind." It wasn't until I was drugged and raped by a colleague in my own home that I finally understood the meaning behind that quote. I now see it as using discernment when someone is giving me their opinion or advice. I also recognized that the shouting, loudest voice in my head is my ego. My ego is a record of the past; it does not know the future because it has never been there before. It likes the familiar, which is how I kept re-creating the same scenarios by listening to that voice telling me I needed a man.

I was journaling one day and asked my guides and angels to increase the volume of my intuition so I could hear it better. I wanted to turn up the volume so I would not make the same mistakes moving forward. I wanted my intuition to be louder than the obnoxious attention-seeking addict voice in my head, aka my ego, telling me I needed male attention. What I wrote next blew my mind. I wrote: "Your intuition does not need to be louder; you need to quiet your ego to hear it." So it wasn't about the loudest voice; it was about hearing the inner voice. Wow, that was a life-changing moment for me. To get quiet and to go within to hear my inner guidance.

A few years later, when it was under new leadership, I received a call from an old friend who was now the association's new chapter president. He had been there when I originally presented the idea about the Stand by You committee. He asked me to send him all the work I had done. He wanted to reintroduce the committee to the board, as he was an ally and hoped to create social change while serving on the board. Unfortunately, it went nowhere, and the Stand by You committee was once again buried. However, the fact that a Black male colleague was willing to risk his status had given me a glimpse of hope that change can happen. Eventually, like a scale, one person can be the difference and tilt it!

I had justified ignoring my intuition about staying away from Richard and again bought into my drug of choice: the age-old story of women using our looks and bodies to persuade men to help us get what we want. I paid a high price to learn a valuable lesson. I learned that the old social norms—the loud patriarchal voices that tell women of all ages that we need a man to survive—needs to be silenced. We need to create a more powerful voice for women, one that shouts a narrative of empowerment and being able to support ourselves so we can speak our truths and live lives that align with who we really are.

Just like my old oak tree, I have weathered many storms, and I am still standing. My hope in sharing this story is not to make you feel sorry for me or to judge me. It is so we can learn and grow together. I own my mistakes, I have sought therapy, and I have and will continue to use my experiences and lessons learned to educate myself and others. By sharing my story, I can finally speak my truth. It is me taking my voice back, including the loudest one in my head. And you can too.

CHAPTER SIX

AM I DATING A NARCISSIST?

In October 2019, I was finding my stride in my new city of Tampa and building my communication coaching and consulting business. I was even starting to recover from the emotional wounds of my assault. I was renting a room from a dear friend and colleague while I was looking for my "just right" new neighborhood. Her townhome overlooked a lake. I was enjoying my coffee and the lake when I got a message from a friend who knew I loved Andrea Bocelli. They told me that tickets were on sale for his famous Valentine's Day concert in Tampa!

I decided to purchase a ticket to take myself to the concert. My friend asked why I bought only one ticket. "What if you are in a relationship by then? What would you do?" I told them I had waited years to be in a relationship to go to this event and didn't want to depend on a man to make it happen. I also told them that if I ended up in a relationship, they could either buy a ticket, upgrade our tickets, or celebrate the holiday on a different day, and I would still go as planned.

I felt inspired and independent and that my life was finally going in a positive direction. That is, until November 19, 2019, when I again got a call from the hospital in North Carolina that my dad was in bad shape and that I should get to North Carolina as soon as possible. I packed my car, got on the road about nine p.m., and drove through the night.

My dad passed away a few days later. My mom was in a wheelchair, and my dad had been her primary care provider. It was decided that since I didn't have children living at home with me and I owned my own company, it would make the most sense that I take care of my mom in North Carolina until my brother could relocate her to Pennsylvania with him. While my siblings stayed with my mom after my dad's funeral, I drove back to Florida over the Thanksgiving holiday to pack up my stuff, either putting it in storage, giving it away, or taking it back to North Carolina with me.

I am grateful for the time I had taking care of my mom. It was healing in many ways, but if you have ever been a caretaker, you know it is exhausting. I was washing and changing my mom, cooking, cleaning, doing laundry, and handling my dad's estate issues. Nothing was in my mom's name, so when my dad passed, all her money and income stopped. She didn't even have a credit card at age eighty-five; she was only authorized on my dad's account. When she slept, I worked remotely on my consulting/coaching business. I was hardly getting any sleep. I was mentally, physically, and spiritually exhausted.

My dad had passed just a few weeks shy of their sixty-fifth anniversary. My mom was sad, lonely, and lost without him. Given her state of mind, I was trying to keep the house as normal as possible until she left for Pennsylvania. Rather than trying to sell all the items myself after mom left, I was referred to Jack, who bought estates to resell in his thrift store. My mom and I made an appointment with him to review the house's items. He was charming, and it was obvious he was short and a smoker, and we learned he's divorced and two of his six children are still living at home. My mom swore we were flirting. I argued we definitely were *not* (he is so not my type!), but it had been a nice change of pace from my new day-to-day caregiver responsibilities. He lived around the corner and offered to help should we need anything.

A few weeks later, I took him up on his offer and asked for help removing an old recliner that was blocking mom's access to the porch. The weather was beautiful for December in North Carolina, and my mom wanted to sit outside on the patio and color. We both loved coloring and found it was very relaxing. Since my mom's hands were no longer steady enough for her other forms of artwork, coloring brought her comfort and distracted her from the emotions of losing my dad and moving. Within minutes, Jack was at my mom's house, taking the chair apart and carrying it out to his truck. I was impressed with how he ripped the chair in half and threw it over his shoulder. I remember thinking that was hot! Okay, little man, I see you. I offered to pay him for his help, but he refused, saying, "Buy me a beer one day."

In early 2020, the ambulance came to transport my mom to Pennsylvania. With my mom gone, it was time to get the house ready to sell. Shortly after she left, Jack and his dad came to remove the home's contents. It was a hectic, emotional morning between my mom leaving, not having had time to mourn the loss of my dad, Jack and his dad packing and moving out all the furniture and other items, the cleaning crew's arrival—while I was also dealing with a difficult client and had to leave on a red-eye flight to Florida on a business trip the following day. The only furniture being left in the house was my bed, which had to be moved to the kitchen after the cleaning crew left, to prepare for the next day's carpet cleaners. I would return to North Carolina until my mom's house sold.

Jack offered to come back later that night to help me move the bed into the kitchen. After we moved it, he said, "You can take me for that beer now." (I know, you're already thinking, *Noooo*). I was beyond tired and still needed to pack, so I asked him if we could wait until I came back, but he wouldn't take no for an answer. Once again, I leaned into my people-pleasing tendency and agreed to go out even though I was mentally and physically exhausted.

We had a lot of fun at a local bar. We laughed and had a good conversation. It was a great distraction from the emotions and chaos of the day. He took me home, then helped me pack for my trip. We talked right up to when I needed to leave for the airport. As I got ready, he made coffee and started my car so it would be warm when I got in. It felt nice to have someone take care of me. (You're breathing a sigh of relief, right?)

But not so fast. That night led me into a whirlwind of a relationship that has forever changed me. My intent in sharing this experience is to pull back the curtain on unhealthy relationships, expose the controlling, manipulative, frightening, and downright scary behavior I experienced, and share the lessons I have extracted that led me to making one of the boldest positive choices of my life.

WHEN I HAD SAID MY PREDAWN THANK-YOU AND GOODBYE TO JACK TO catch my red-eye to Florida to facilitate a communication training for a client, I was depleted. I barely made it through that day. Between the client being difficult, fighting off a cold, the mental and physical exhaustion of caring for my mom, and staying up all night made this one of the most challenging trainings I have ever done. While I was in Florida for this trip, I would also need to look for a new apartment for when I eventually resumed my life in Tampa.

During my business trip, I found it odd that I often thought of the short man in North Carolina since he wasn't someone I would consider as a potential romantic partner. I wanted a man who was tall, a nonsmoker, with no children or pets, and wanted to travel. My friends teased me about him, but I assured them it was just a fun night and I would be headed back to Florida once my mom's house was sold. Jack and I had been texting, and he kept telling me that I would not need an apartment in Florida. He was convinced I would stay with him. I was not.

Upon my return to North Carolina, Jack stood in the airport to welcome me back. We went out and had a nice dinner. When I arrived at my mother's house, I discovered that the internet had been disconnected. Seeing as how I was trying to run my business remotely, this was a huge problem. I was very upset. Jack offered to let me use his Wi-Fi, but I insisted on getting my own, which I did. Over the following weeks, he told me I didn't need the Wi-Fi because I would end up living with him. I laughed it off as I was sure I would be driving back home to Florida when my mom's house was sold.

In early February 2020, my mom's house had a buyer. It was only a matter of weeks before I could head back home to Tampa. I had been dating Jack on almost a daily basis. I stayed at his house more than my mom's. He would remind me every chance he got of "I told you that you didn't need to get your own Wi-Fi, if only you had listened to me." He also kept saying he hoped the deal on my mother's house would fall through so I would stay longer and realize I was going to end up with him. Unbeknownst to me at the time, this is called "grooming" or "conditioning," a subtle technique often used to break people down and recondition them. Did I mention that Jack had served in the military as an officer for over twenty years, where he certainly had experience with reconditioning soldiers?

Valentine's Day was around the corner, and I had my ticket to see Andrea Bocelli in concert in Tampa. My friend's fear became my reality; I wasn't just dating someone but living in a different state! But I kept my promise to myself and booked a plane ticket back to Florida to spend Valentine's Day with Andrea!

Jack and I decided to celebrate Valentine's Day the night before. We went to one of my favorite restaurants. We ate incredible food, enjoyed tasty cocktails, and laughed until we got home. Jack went out to smoke a cigarette, and I headed into the bedroom and changed into sexy lingerie. I waited for Jack to come to bed, but I fell asleep crying. He apparently ended up on the phone with his oldest daughter while he smoked and drank himself into oblivion. It was almost two a.m. before he ping-ponged himself off the walls (unbeknownst to me, this was an ordinary affair for him) and fell into bed. I lay there hurt and crying. He was supposed to take me to the airport at five a.m.

I got out of bed, took my luggage, and headed to my mom's house.

I lay in the empty, dark house, shedding tears of pain and embarrassment. I secretly hoped that he would wake up and realize I was gone and come to find me and take me to the airport, but that never happened. I drove myself to the airport and boarded the plane.

I cried most of the flight, and once again, I had allowed this man to keep me up all night before an important event. I landed in Tampa, and when I turned on my phone, there was a plethora of messages from Jack. I didn't have time to answer them as my dear friend Connie picked me up. It was a whirlwind of a day. I had jammed it so full of visits with friends that Connie and I ran from one appointment to the next. I was so tired and pressed for time all day that I even forgot to call my mom and wish her a happy birthday. Connie, her partner, and I had an amazing dinner before they dropped me off at the concert arena.

When I got to the concert, the ticket person asked me, "Just one?" She looked at me with sympathy and pity, like it was sad to be there all alone. I told her proudly, "Yes, just me; I couldn't have asked for better company!" Once I found my seat, I collapsed in exhaustion. Andrea was getting over a cold, and since he had canceled all the other concerts before this one, I tried to turn my disappointment at how little he sang into gratitude for finally making my dream into a reality. But the truth is, I was disappointed. I was once again exhausted mentally and physically, which enhanced my disappointment, not just about the concert but also with myself.

To top it off, while in Florida, I learned that the sale of my mother's house had fallen out of contract. I was confused. Part of me wanted to be done and move back to Florida, and the other half wanted more time to explore my relationship with Jack even though the pre-Valentine's Day shenanigans should have ended our relationship. Let's be honest, in hindsight the relationship should never have gotten that far to begin with.

Once again, when I got back to the airport in North Carolina, Jack was waiting for me. Since my car was parked there, he'd had his dad drop him off at the airport. That way we could drive home together. He knew I loved the show *The Bachelor*, and he signaled to me to do the famous "run and jump hug" that all the women candidates do when approaching the bachelor. A nearby bystander commented on how romantic and adorable we were (if she only knew the story). Jack apologized for Valentine's Day, and we grabbed a bite to eat. During dinner, I told him how the offer on my mom's house had fallen through. He was happy and said it gave him more time to convince me to stay there with him.

At some point, I moved in with Jack, and we did have fun, especially in the beginning. We loved to take long rides on his motorcycle, visit our favorite restaurants, have family nights with his parents and kids where I would make dinner, and we would play games afterward. I often find myself drawn to men with large or close families as I always desired that as being security. Everywhere we went people adored us! Maybe it was the drastic difference in our heights, especially if I wore my high heels. I would be almost a foot taller than Jack. I posted photos of our good moments on social media. Everyone oohed and aahed over our relationship. All my friends were baffled that I would date a man who not only had kids but was shorter than me, had a dog, smoked—and that I was willing to put my world travel plans on hold! All my previous Wish List items for a relationship—tall, nonsmoking, childless, loved travel—were being ignored for what appeared to the public as a perfect relationship.

Because we looked so Facebook fabulous, I was encouraged by a TEDx event coordinator to apply to speak about how I turned my deal-breakers into a magical relationship. The idea I presented was about how our conscious bias could interfere with life's possibilities. I would use the analogy of dating apps to highlight how we disregard people for our conscious bias about height, weight, age, race, etc. I was elated at first when I was told I was indeed selected to share this idea from the TEDx stage. Preparing a TEDx talk takes anywhere from three months to a year. Over the next several months I would work on my script and presentation.

One day Jack again reminded me he'd told me that I should've just listened to him from the start. "I told you, you didn't need Wi-Fi, and you didn't. I told you that you would not need an apartment in

Florida, and you didn't. I am always right." This conversation was a pivotal conversation. What I did not know then was that he was continuing to condition, or groom, me.

Have you ever heard the story about the frog and the cook? The cook sweetly invites the frog to swim in a pot of warm water. The frog trusts what appears to be a kind and charismatic person and jumps into the pot and swims around, thinking its life is great. All along, the cook is slowly turning up the heat. Before the frog could realize the water was boiling, the frog was dinner. That was exactly what happened as our so-called fairy tale unraveled.

Our relationship was starting to show deeper cracks. Jack drank daily and often stumbled into bed before nine p.m. He also had the habit of saying awful things to me and his children. The next day he would have no recollection of his actions. We would argue about his drinking, but he would always throw in my face that the very first night we went out—the night my mom left (while I was physically, mentally, and emotionally exhausted)—that he had told me then that he drank every night. Which meant that he was honest, and I had no reason to complain. What that taught me was that I needed to ask better questions! When he said he drank every night, I thought a beer or two, no problem, but to get piss drunk and pass out almost every night is a whole different story. And now I should be ashamed because I knew? It somehow had become my fault! This is very common in controlling, abusive relationships.

The water got turned up quickly for me on March 16, 2020, as I sat at my desk and watched email after email pour in, canceling all my scheduled upcoming consulting work events. The year 2020 would have been my best because of all the work that was on the calendar, but when COVID-19 broke out and the world started to shut down, I watched my business go down the drain with every incoming cancellation. At the time I didn't know to have contractual clauses for world pandemics. I was not qualified, or so I was told by Jack, to receive unemployment. It was the perfect storm. Most controlling relationships want to create a dependency, so my business struggling from an outside circumstance that I had no control over played right into

Jack's hands. Plus he didn't need to isolate me, as I already had no friends or family in North Carolina. And COVID sealed the deal on my creating new relationships because we all went on lockdown for the next year.

Jack once again took this opportunity to tell me that at least I'd stayed with him. Imagine if I had returned to Florida and had to pay rent; how would I survive without him? That played right into my addiction. I was concerned about pulling my own weight, but he assured me that all I did for him and his family was far more valuable to him than any income I could produce. (Remember this moment because in the next chapter you will drop your jaw at what he tells me later.) It was true I did a lot for Jack and his family. His dad had cancer, and his care was difficult for his mother. Jack would stay over at their home to help after the surgery. I cooked dinner for his parents and our family every night. I cared for the house, the dog, and Jack's two younger children who lived with us. I would cover at his thrift store and sell furniture when I wasn't cooking, cleaning, or running errands for him—and his kids.

In late August, Jack's son was having a birthday party. He had friends sleeping over when Jack got totally shit-faced. We ended up arguing and he threw me out, in front of his son and his friends. He literally started taking my belongings and putting them outside. I was mortified. Because it brought up old emotional wounds of when my mom would throw me out, I was shaken to my core. Jack eventually passed out and I (hardly) slept on the couch. The next morning, he acted like nothing had happened. Because I was so fearful about what I would do and where I would go, I ended up staying. Remember we were still in quarantine, on lockdown, including my business. And if that wasn't awful enough, the next day I went to his thrift store and covered for him so he could take his son and all his friends to play paintball. As luck would have it, the van broke down on the way. They ended up getting to the paintball place somehow but needed a ride home. Yup, you guessed it. I closed the store and drove his truck over an hour away to pick them up.

Our relationship was extremely toxic. What people didn't see on social media was the emotional and mental abuse and control. After one of our fights, I found out that Jack was tracking my phone. I had gone out for a drive to clear my head, and when I came home, he asked me if I had called my ex-boyfriend, Wayne, again. Wayne was someone I had previously dated off and on; he wasn't a good fit as a life partner, but we made great friends. I said no and asked him what he meant by the comment. Jack told me he knew that after the last time we fought, I had spoken to Wayne for an hour on the phone. Wow! That was when I found out that Jack was tracking my phone calls and text messages. And that was just the beginning of it.

Jack would create what is called triangulations between me and his oldest daughter, his ex-wife, and anyone else he could pit against each other. Creating triangulations is another technique used in controlling relationships. It creates an emotional imbalance in the victims, which is important in keeping the abuser's control over the relationships. On top of his constant drinking and smoking, Jack also controlled most of my finances. Although he did pay all the house expenses, which he was doing prior to me moving in and sharing a bed and a few feet of closet space, I was paying all my own personal expenses, such as my car and health insurance, as well as all my business expenses like maintenance of my website, calendar and database subscriptions, etc. Money was another way he could control me. If I behaved, I would get rewarded with mani/pedicures on our Sunday fun days, or he would leave cash in the drawer for me to get my nails done or to take his kids out for special treats like Starbucks or Chick-fil-A. Since I wasn't doing any consulting, while I was "bringing in so much value to" Jack and his family during the pandemic, I had to tap into my savings from the sale of my home. He could easily manipulate me. He knew I had huge fears about money and lack of it, and he used it to his advantage. Remember, when I sold my home, I had paid off all my debts, and I wanted to keep it that way.

At times I would have thoughts that, once again, I was giving up my dreams of traveling in exchange for the security of being with a man, which I deeply felt I needed. It was my addiction after all. I slowly dissolved into Jack's world. My dreams of traveling turned into waiting for Jack's youngest children to graduate so we could tailgate at all the Miami Dolphins football games by taking an RV and following them for the season. Like the frog in the pot, I chose the appearance of comfort and ease and was oblivious to my slowly increasing discomfort. Again, I exchanged my dream of international travel to wait four years so I could travel by RV and sit in a parking lot. Not even go into the stadium to watch the games! I have always been a lightweight drinker, and football has never been my hobby, nor was drinking all day, especially in parking lots. What the hell was I doing?

By now my body was in a constant state of flight, fight, freeze, and fawn, and it started to show in my physical health. I found myself once again needing iron infusions because my iron was deathly low. Because I am allergic to iron, I needed to have a special concoction of drugs to keep me alive while getting the iron transfusions—which made me sick and groggy for hours after each treatment. I am highly sensitive to any drugs, which is why when drugged during my assault I was lucky not to be killed from the dose alone. Not to mention the expense because my insurance did not cover all the cost.

True to my form, I had powered on and written and published my first book that I cowrote with my mentor at the time on communication and conflict. Which was the first time Jack stole my spotlight by ordering the first copy of my book and then doing an unboxing video of himself opening my book! Like the frog, at the time I didn't realize what he was doing; I was so flattered that he wanted the first copy I didn't realize he had stolen a once-in-a-lifetime first book reveal from me!

The next thing that happened, in November, was that I dislocated my jaw and needed surgery to have it fixed. I had been so stressed that I was grinding my teeth in my sleep. Since it was still during COVID, I had to wait weeks for an appointment. Once again, it was very expensive as my insurance did not cover all the fees. On top of that, over the holidays I could not eat the delicious food I was making for everyone else. All of this was adding to my emotional and financial stress. Not once did Jack offer to help me with my own personal expenses.

As I was preparing my TEDx talk for the next month, I was struggling with it as I realized that, although I did believe deeply in not using our conscious bias to miss out on opportunities, I did feel like I was living a lie because I was in relationship hell. I thought about removing myself from the lineup of speakers, but I didn't want anyone to know the truth about my fairy-tale relationship being only a myth. I justified doing my talk because at that time—after George Floyd's murder and other national events—I felt that the topic was timely and important. So I took the stage anyway.

While I was on stage publicly declaring my love for this man, in the real world we were on the brink of our relationship crumbling as I started to awaken to my truth. That talk would be forever in cyberspace (or so I thought): a record of me completely disregarding my core values in pursuit of a fairy tale. And if that wasn't bad enough, he stole my spotlight once again by convincing the TEDx team to allow him to come on stage and propose to me at the close of my talk!

My son, Johnny, was in the audience yelling, *You better say yes, Mom*. My friends were all screaming. It was tremendous pressure, and I did say yes, but what everyone watching didn't know was the emotional war behind the picture I had painted on Facebook of rainbows and unicorns. After our very public engagement, our private relationship got worse.

Immediately after his public proposal, Jack told me we could not discuss anything related to the wedding for at least thirty days. Friends and family excited about our new engagement bombarded me with questions about the big day. I didn't want anyone to know that Jack had told me that topic was off-limits, so I felt myself crawling inside and shrinking with each inquiry. Typically, when a couple gets engaged, there is excitement around the next steps, yet I was forbidden to even mention it.

After a month of waiting, we finally started to talk about a potential wedding, and that was when the roller-coaster ride of emotions went off the tracks. When we started talking about the wedding, we would fight. Jack would find a way to make it my fault every time. I was so dizzy from our arguments and the gaslighting that I started to gaslight and question myself! Then he would set me up to look like a crazy person, and I would step right into his plot. He would tell people stories about me that were not true. Then he would pick fights with me in front of people, and because I literally was going crazy, I would respond with anger, hence validating his story. The final straw was when we went out to dinner one night and he brought up the wedding and then made a very public scene arguing with me and accusing me of fighting with him when I drink (which is called projection: accusing someone else of the very thing you do). I told him that night we would not discuss any marriage plans moving forward.

When journaling in the days after, I asked myself, "Am I dating a narcissist?" I called my dear friend Carole, who had stayed with us during my trip to Florida to give my TEDx talk, and I shared with her the question I had asked myself. "Now that you have asked," Carole responded, "*yes*, you are." She didn't want to tell me before I came to it on my terms, knowing I would push her away and defend Jack. She had been patiently waiting for me to realize it. We concluded that I needed some time away from him to figure out what I wanted and what I would do next.

CHAPTER SEVEN

A FORK IN THE ROAD

After my conversation with Carole, I decided I needed to step off the merry-go-round and get some alone time to clear my head. I wanted to take a road trip to visit my friends back in Florida. That trip turned from a solo trip to Jack convincing me to make it a girls' trip by taking his teenage daughter. We had taken girls' trips in the past, and while I love her, I wanted this trip for myself, but since Jack was controlling my purse strings, I said yes. Days later, Jack told me I should also take his younger son, also a teen, who was also living with us. Wait... What? *So now, instead of me getting away to clear my head, now I have both your children, and you are the one who gets the vacation?* How did this happen? It happened because of my addiction and my belief that I needed him to be safe and secure. Ironically, I didn't feel safe or secure.

That trip to Florida with his children was very eye-opening! We went to an amusement park in Tampa. When we got there, Jack texted me, saying he saw we were there and to have fun. I asked the kids how he knew we were there. That was when his son told me that Jack has an app that tracks all of us. All of a sudden, the picture became clear! It now made sense: the days he would question me where I was and what I did, he already knew what I had done and was testing me. Wow, that felt even more violating than him tracking my phone calls. Yet again, this was only the tip of the iceberg of what he was doing without my knowledge.

In addition to finding out how intrusive Jack was, I also experienced challenges with the kids during our trip. Although there were a few, the ones worth mentioning were when his daughter refused to listen to my advice about putting on sunscreen while we were at the beach, and we suffered from her sun poisoning. I say we because I stayed up with her all night and cared for her. We hardly got any rest before returning for our long car ride to North Carolina. Then, while driving home, Jack's son challenged my authority. I was so enraged that I pulled the car over on the side of I-95 to address his behavior. My own children never disrespected me that way. I would be damned if I was going to let someone else's. The rest of the car ride was filled with tension.

When we got home, I still had not gotten the time I needed to process all that was happening around me. Jack had placed flower petals all over the bedroom, with candles and a card. He knew that trip was a result of his pushing me away, so he had to once again turn on the love-bombing to reel me back in. I later learned how abusers use your desires to manipulate you. But I had wanted time for myself to think and hear my thoughts without all the drama that kept me off-balance and in alignment with the story he was telling people about "crazy" me. So when my best friend Shelly was going to cancel a bucket list trip of her husband's to do the Dragon's Tail by motorcycle in South Carolina because her beautiful Great Dane, Rogue, was sick and needed someone to care for him, I jumped at the opportunity to create a win/win. I told her I would return to Florida and take care of Rogue! Shelly is my family; she and her husband have supported me through my divorce, many moves, and all my life challenges. This was an opportunity not only to be there when they needed me but to create space for me to get clear in my head.

Jack was not happy about my decision to go to Florida again. In his mind I had just had a vacation. This trip was not up for negotia-tion; I was going. The spending money he would usually keep in the drawer disappeared in the week leading up to my trip. It was clear to me that if I did not behave in a way he liked, one of my forms of punishment was that he would cut off my allowance. At that point, my business was somewhat alive again but not generating much income, my bank funds were becoming depleted, and my credit cards were accumulating debt. I decided that I had credit, and if I had to take on more debt to clear my head, it was a small price to pay.

The night before my solo trip to Florida, Jack got drunk (again) and started a fight with me. I knew it was only a matter of time before he passed out, so I did my best not to engage. The next morning, I wanted to get on the road early, but Jack begged me to stay and work out our argument from the night before. Miraculously, he somehow finally remembered his drunken behavior. After allowing him to delay my trip for a couple of hours and listening to his pleading for me not to go, I got in the car and left.

Shortly after I started to drive, I got a text from him. "Please don't go, come home." That was when I heard a loud voice in my head say, "Don't you fucking turn around! You keep FUCKING DRIVING!" The voice repeated that over and over again, louder each time. So I did keep on fucking driving, and by an hour into my trip, as I got onto Highway I-95, a sense of relief washed over me. My body released its tension, and the tears came shortly after.

I met my dear friend Robin for dinner that night. She told me something I will never forget. She said, "You will never live out your dreams of global travel if you stay in this relationship." She said that if his kids ever did move out, we would most likely do Jack's tailgating adventure, but shortly after, we would return to North Carolina, and I would go from caring for his kids to caring for his elderly parents, never fulfilling any of my dreams. That really landed for me, clari-fying that I was choosing to live Jack's dream, not my own.

I spent the next week with Rogue, and I would tell him that this was our mutual healing retreat. We both needed some love and atten-tion. I brought my Human Design report to review and remind myself of what I was up to in my life's plan. The time alone gave me space to calm my system and finally be quiet enough to hear my own thoughts. It gave me room to take a serious inventory of what was really going on in my relationship.

After my week with Rogue, I went to spend a few days with my friend Carole, who was going to help me create a safe exit strategy from the relationship with Jack and get me back to living in Florida. The threefold plan was for me to go back to North Carolina and find a way to get my phone back on my own plan to mitigate Jack's intrusive behavior, get a job so I could start saving money, and go back home to Florida safely and as quickly as possible.

It seemed like a great plan, but Jack always seemed to be one step ahead of me somehow. But how? That question was soon answered when one day I got locked out of my MacBook Pro. I was frantic! All my intellectual property for my business and writing was in that computer. Jack told me it wasn't a big deal, that we would just get a new computer, but to me it was my life. When I called my computer tech guy who could remotely tap into my computer, he asked me, "Are you alone?" I told him I was in my office by myself, but Jack and the kids were in the other room. He then asked me, "Are you safe?" He went on to explain that the only way my computer could have been locked was from someone who had the password to access it. Now it all made sense. Not only was Jack tracking my phone calls and physical location but had access to all my email, computer files, and social media. Everything he was doing was intentional. Since then, while writing this book, I have discovered that he also read my handwritten journals.

I knew then it was crucial to seriously implement my exit plan ASAP. I got a job bartending at a bar owned by Jack's close friend, working at night when Jack was home so his youngest daughter would not be alone. I was scheduled to start the Monday after Mother's Day. On Mother's Day, we took a motorcycle ride to my favorite restaurant for brunch. He even took me to buy shoes for my new job. I thought he supported my new job, but Jack was only playing the game of appearing supportive to his family and friends. I had no idea what anger was brewing inside him. My new job equaled a threat to his control. Before we headed home to get ready for dinner with his parents and children, he made a random stop. When we got off the bike, I asked him where we were. He would not tell me but asked me to follow him. He led me into one of the most beautiful event halls I had ever seen. It had vaulted ceilings and huge windows that over-looked an incredible view of a forest and lake.

Jack took me down to the water and showed me the outside area where, he explained, our wedding ceremony could take place with the lake as the backdrop. I was shocked and pissed! First of all, this place was exactly what I had wanted, but he never mentioned its exis-tence until that moment. And secondly, I'd told him after our last public argument that I no longer wanted to discuss any wedding plans. And just when I thought it couldn't be any worse, he dropped to one knee and asked me again to marry him. He said—without all the people, without the stage spotlight—"Tell me now, will you marry me?" He knew that integrity is my number one core value and that I would not lie. I tried to make light of it and told him to stop being silly and to get up. But he was dead serious, and he wanted me to say yes again. But I just couldn't bring myself to say yes, especially since I'd had time to step away and really see our relationship without my drug dealer (aka my ego) telling me I needed a man and marriage. All I said was to remind him that we'd agreed not to talk about this right now.

His mood changed that second, and I knew he was mad. It was one of the most uncomfortable motorcycle rides home, not because of the ride but the conditions. The tension was so thick you could cut it with a knife. We got ready and went to dinner with his family, which then turned up the heat of being uncomfortable. He was rude to me, and even his mother said something. When we got home, he gave me the cold-shoulder treatment, which he knew I hated.

The next morning, Monday, was just as awkward. Jack left for work without much communication. That night would be my first shift at my new bartending gig. I didn't want to upset the apple cart anymore, so I made sure dinner was prepared ahead of time. When he got home, all he had to do was open the crockpot and feed himself and the kids. Later that afternoon, as I was getting ready to leave for my first shift, he sprang it on me that he needed me to pick his daughter up from school. What? I had to go to work and didn't want to be late on my first day. But I did it anyhow because my fear of his retaliation was much greater. I rushed to pick her up and took her to his store. He got in my car, and we had a huge fight over "my attitude."

I barely made it to my new job on time, and I was shaken physically, mentally, and emotionally. But my inner event planner kicked in once again, and I sucked it up. I made it through my first night of bartending. I headed home without knowing what I was about to walk into. I was greeted with the silent treatment, followed by passive-aggressive remarks. When I addressed Jack's remarks, he let me have it, and I mean have it. He told me that I added no value to him or his family. Everything he had said previously about being aware of all that I did—the cooking, cleaning, driving, helping his parents, his store—had added value to him and his family, he was now saying the opposite. And then he did it again: he verbally threw me out of the house, saying I had to be out in the morning! His children were home, and his daughter heard the entire conversation. In that moment I knew I had a choice to make. I could commit to a life like my mom had—taking care of everyone else, dealing with a controlling partner and never having peace, not fulfilling her dreams and purpose, only to grow older with health challenges that led her to be chairbound for the rest of her life—or I could jump without a parachute not knowing how it would unfold. This time I didn't worry about what I would do or where I was going. I got in my car, went to Walmart, and bought moving boxes. I immediately returned and stayed up the whole night packing, and when I was not packing, I cried and prayed. It was another long, sleepless, scary night, but I knew I was at a fork in the road.

The next morning, Jack woke up and was sweet as pie. He even made me coffee and we agreed to end things. Holy shit, the emotional whiplash can keep a person off-balance. We came up with a plan to tell everyone that we'd decided to take a break to preserve our relationship. He took me to his parents' house, where we told them this story. Then we told the kids, his and mine, the same thing. He offered to help move me back to Florida. He told me I could take the office furniture he'd bought for me. When I responded as if I was shocked (because I was), his response was that I could take all the gifts he'd bought me since after all, they were gifts. In that instant I remembered something Carole had advised when she was helping me create my plan to leave. At that time I was resistant to hear it, but now in hindsight it was excellent advice. She told me that I had sacrificed so much for Jack and his family over the past year and a half, and since I would be starting from scratch all over again, that I should take everything I could of value that he allowed me.

It was because I heard her words in my head that I quickly responded, "Even Lady G?" Lady G was a Honda Shadow 1100 motorcycle. He was shocked. I said, "Well, you did gift her to me for my birthday." He had won my motorcycle in an auction. He had promised me we would go register it together, but one day I came home and she had a license plate tag. When I asked him if he titled it in my name, he said no, that he had to go for something else and while he was already there, he went ahead and transferred the title to his name and got the tag for it so I could start riding. He made it seem like it was no big deal, but to me it was! If it was a gift, it should have been titled in my name. I did get to take Lady G back to Florida with me.

The next big thing up for negotiation was my engagement ring. Since he was kicking me out, he ended the relationship. Traditionally, if the giver breaks off the engagement, the receiver gets to keep the ring. With Carole's advice in my ear and the reality that I was heading back to Florida with next to nothing, everything counted. Jack would brag about how brightly my ring shone when it landed on my hand. When I brought it to the jeweler to be cleaned the first time, the woman servicing me didn't seem as impressed as I thought she might be when I handed it to her. I remember thinking it was odd.

As my day to leave quickly approached, Jack offered to purchase the ring from me. I was shocked, but I put on my business hat and negotiated. We agreed that he would give me $2,000 for the ring. I thought that was a very generous offer since I would most likely not get that much from selling it to a pawn shop when I got back to Florida. I also did not want to deal with the emotional weight of taking it from place to place, trying to get the best deal, so I accepted his offer. I still don't know the reason behind his offer. Maybe the ring was worth more, or perhaps it wasn't real and he wanted to keep up the appearance of being a big spender and generous nice guy. People who have narcissistic tendencies will do anything to protect their assets and appearances. Either way, I took the deal. Jack then would use that against me as he later told everyone I was a gold digger and my receiving a payout for the ring was his proof. If I was a gold digger, I was certainly not very good at picking wealthy men! My final "haul" of $2,000, two office shelves, and a motorcycle hardly helped me get started again. First and last month's rent and a security deposit alone were more than that.

Over the next several days with Jack, it was like walking on eggshells, and it wreaked havoc on my nervous system. I did my best to please Jack and keep up the appearance that everything was normal. I cared for the kids and house and cooked meals as if nothing was happening. I would pack when I was home alone, and I did my best not to engage with Jack. We had planned to head back to Florida the next week, as he had to get coverage for the store to help me move back. You're probably wondering why I had agreed to let him help me. I let him help me because he had a truck and trailer, and if I tried to do it myself, I would have to pay a mover and that would have taken the little resources I had. Plus I felt he deserved to be inconvenienced after everything I had gone through with him. I can only guess that he agreed to move me back to keep up his "good guy" appearance. I counted the days until we would leave—and then there was a gas shortage in North Carolina. Jack postponed our trip, then changed his mind. One minute we were going; the next, we were not. It was like he was turning on and off a light switch, and every flick created more anxiety within me. I knew, and so did he, that if I was emotionally off-balance, I was vulnerable. He told me at one point that we could just offload the trailer, and I could stay instead of leaving. I told him—playing the part because, at that point, my main goal was getting back to Florida safely—that if we ever planned to be together again, this move back to Florida was essential. The minute I surrendered to his emotional game of stop and go, he decided we would leave the next day.

We got on the road the following day, and when we did stop for gas the first time, we ended up in a long line waiting, but after that, we had no issues with gas. After driving all day, our first stop was at the warehouse where I rented a storage space and unloaded my belongings for temporary storage. We then went to the hotel where Jack and I would stay overnight. Yes, you read that right! I agreed to stay with him the night before he headed back to North Carolina. In hindsight, I realize how stupid that was.

After checking into the hotel, we decided to grab dinner at the Chili's chain restaurant within walking distance. My son Johnny joined us for dinner. Jack was sucking down pints of beer like a person who was just rescued after days of being lost in a hot desert. After dinner, as soon as we got outside, Jack started throwing up all over the parking lot. I was able to walk us back to the hotel, where Jack passed out. The next morning, he was up before six, dressed, and didn't have much to say. We checked out of the hotel, and he got in his truck and drove off. That was the last time I would see Jack in person.

However, he and I talked occasionally after I left. We both played into keeping up the facade of potentially getting back together. For Jack, I was sure it was to keep up his "good guy" appearance; for me, it was about keeping myself safe. He would take any opportunity to jab me verbally. I was staying with my dear friend Shelly, as she and her husband (and Rogue) had agreed to let me stay with them for a month so I could get on my feet. They had set up the guest room to include a desk so I could work and gotten an office chair from an auction. But they did not realize it had been infested with bed bugs. I woke up the next morning with bites all over me. When I shared that experience with Jack and asked his advice on getting rid of them (being a thrift store owner, he had experience with checking and cleaning used items to prevent this very situation), he was smug and told me that I deserved it and was not at all helpful in resolving my issue.

On the night of May 27, 2021, while sleeping with Rogue on the couch since my room was being exterminated, I decided that my earlier conversation with Jack would be our last. I was going to do my own extermination. I would not give him the opportunity to make me feel demeaned again. At some point after making my decision to leave Jack, when I had a clear mind, I had made lists of our shared contacts on social media, email, and phone. I had sealed the lists in envelopes that had fake titles on the outside. I waited until after nine p.m. when I knew Jack would be passed out, grabbed the envelopes, and started severing my ties to all connections between us. I went on Facebook and blocked everyone, including his children; I deleted every post related to Jack. I didn't need Facebook to remind me of him. Then email, then my phone. I knew the only way to heal truly was to cut off all and any possible communication with him. I felt terrible about abandoning his children, especially his youngest, but it was time that I put myself first.

Because integrity was/is my number one personal core value, I had put honoring my word over my well-being. I now realize that integrity starts with me first and prioritizing my emotional, mental, and physical wellness. Although I did go along with Jack's public explanation that we were just taking a break in hopes of getting back together one day, I did it to keep me safe from negotiating what I left with to feeling awful for leaving his youngest children. But my responsibility was to myself first.

Putting myself first was a hard lesson to learn for a people-pleasing addict like me. At times it felt deceitful, like I was lying and just a shitty person, but self-care is not selfish! I have been conditioned all my life to fawn over others' requests, especially men's, so it has taken time for me to forgive myself and learn how to have and keep better boundaries.

You've read that as I approached my fiftieth birthday, I faced the fork in the road: I could stay in my current relationship and follow my mother's footsteps, or jump. I made a promise to myself I would do everything I could not to end up in another unhealthy relationship again. It was time for me to take an inward journey and ask myself tough questions, challenge what I considered normal, and learn new tools to change my addictive behavior so I can live the life my heart truly desires. So I jumped, without a parachute, into a journey of recovery and self-exploration, and I am excited to share my process of falling in love with myself and how I now choose *me* before anyone else. And how you can too.

CHAPTER EIGHT

LEAP OF FAITH

Coming back to Florida and not knowing what I would do as I rebuilt my business and my self-confidence—or even where I would live—was uncomfortable for me to be with so many unknowns. But not as uncomfortable as being in an unhealthy relationship. I was dealing with the emotional fallout and repercussions of my relationship with Jack, but I had the comfort of staying at my dear friend Shelly's home for a month to find my footing and rebuild my business. At first I thought I had a great side job bartending in a high-end restaurant and a place to move into, but that quickly fell through, and I had to start the process all over again.

It still amazes me to this day that even though I jumped without a parachute, God, the Universe, Divine, Spirit, or whatever you call it, rose up to meet me. Over the next eight months, as my stay with one friend ended, another opportunity to stay with friends or a house-sitting opportunity showed up. That was when I realized that even though I didn't know where or how I would go, I had the support of the universe and my loving friends, my chosen family.

During that time, I did a lot of self-reflection. My dear friend had introduced me to Julia Cameron's book *The Artist's Way* many years ago. I had carried that book around for years, never daring to open it until 2016. *The Artist's Way,* with its focus on creativity and spirituality and writing daily "morning pages," was a huge tool in my recovery process. I learned how to take myself on weekly "artist dates" and in the process have become excellent at treating myself the way I always wanted the partners in my life to treat me. So much so that I am not easily impressed by men's efforts anymore because I can give myself what I desire; I don't have to look for love and attention from a source other than myself or settle for less than I want.

However, my big takeaway from *The Artist's Way* was the gift of journaling. I dabbled with this ritual in 2016, but in 2017, I became committed to the process, and I have been writing at least three pages a day most days since then. For me, handwriting my thoughts onto paper with a pen has been one of my most therapeutic tools. It allows me to express all the thoughts swirling in my head on paper, where often before I am even done journaling, I have found or uncovered answers to my questions; some were huge aha moments and others just plain peace of mind, without the thoughts swirling in my brain over and over again.

The ritual of journaling, for me, is sacred. It is my direct line to talk with God. When I filled up the pages of one journal with my fears, dreams, and desires, I would add the book to a plastic storage bin. I never wrote the dates on the outside, and there was no rhyme or reason for how I stored the journals. I never intended to go back to read them, but when writing this book in 2024, I wanted to confirm specific dates or events. So one night I took out the storage box and dumped it on my bed to organize the journals. I wrote each book's start and finish dates on the outside and then put them in piles according to the year. When I finished, I went to stack them in chronological order, and that was when I discovered that every book from 2017 to the present was accounted for *except* the books from November 19, 2019, through mid-May 2021. The journals I had been writing in during the time of my relationship with Jack were gone.

I had previously learned that Jack had been reading my journals

—and I had stopped writing in them—when Jack made a comment about something that I hadn't shared with anyone but my journal. It was in that moment that I realized my privacy, even within my journal, had been violated. It wasn't until June 1, 2021, when I got back to Florida and a few days had passed after I had cut him off completely that I finally felt safe enough to write in my journal again. *But I hadn't known until later that he had stolen several of my journals.*

To say I was devastated upon discovering Jack's invasion of my privacy and theft of the journals is an understatement. Just when I thought that man could not hurt me anymore, I found out how selfish he was. Those journals during our time together were not just about him. I was processing my dad's passing, my healing journey with my mom, my challenges of being a caretaker, and so much more. It was like ripping off a scab and jamming salt directly into a wound I thought was healed. It brought me to my knees emotionally as I felt like someone had violated me all over again. The rage was almost unbearable. I knew he had read them, but going to the lengths to steal them was a different story.

IN THE MONTHS AFTER LEAVING JACK, WHILE I WAS REBUILDING MY LIFE in Florida, I learned many things about myself through journaling, especially who I'd been during my relationship with Jack. I now call him my graduation gift. There is a saying that we don't change unless we are in pain, and he helped show me how much pain I was in. I had previously tried to heal my pain with my drug of choice, male attention, and by seeking security through men. I now know that my younger self was screaming for love, attention, and to feel safe. I am no longer a child and can undoubtedly take care of me. I now can make different choices. The bottom line is no one can love me until I do, and no one can make me feel secure. Only I can love and make myself feel safe the way I need to.

I had left Jack, but the emotional withdrawals at times would make me contemplate reaching out to him to get a hit, but just like a person with an addiction, I knew I must resist. When I decided to leave Jack, it was a commitment to myself that I was not willing to break. In Human Design, there is a life cycle called Chiron Return, which occurs around the age of fifty and is connected to the archetype of the "wounded healer." It represents the place of our deepest wounds and the journey of healing that comes with them. I was now fifty and ready to face and heal my deepest wounds. I knew that if I wanted to heal and change generational patterns, not just for me but for my children and my mom, I would have to do the work. Even though I had been exploring my spirituality and doing my work since 2000, when I was introduced to my first coach, Leianne, I knew I would have to take it to the next level of commitment to make lasting changes. I would have to dig down deep and take a hard look at myself, my choices, and my past behaviors. I had to admit that I had a problem and that, indeed, I was addicted to men.

My relationship with Jack also taught me not to enter any relationship, whether with potential mates, friends, or business opportunities, if I am physically, mentally, or emotionally exhausted. When I am tired, I am off-balance. This makes me vulnerable, and unhealthy potential partners look for those opportunities. Most of them are predators and can see a potential target a mile away. It makes someone like me, the addicted people-pleaser, an easy target. Because when I am off-balance, it is easier to control me. We people-pleasers don't tend to see all the red flags when we are not at our best. It does not mean we ask for abuse or look for it. It means we can learn the warnings, care for ourselves, and strengthen our discernment muscles with each opportunity.

Since being in unhealthy relationships was my normal, I had to learn what healthy relationships looked like and how to identify the red flags so I could have awareness to make new choices. Coach Colleen introduced me to the work of Dr. Ramani Suryakantham Durvasula, who is a clinical psychologist who specializes in addressing narcissism. What I love about Dr. Ramani is that she shares her own experiences with narcissistic personality disorder. The way she shares her insights, knowledge, and wisdom was very easy for me to digest. I consumed all her YouTube videos and books. I wanted to make sure I educated myself to make better life choices. Dr. Ramani taught me how to identify red flags, what to say—and what not to say—which is even more important. She also taught me the Gray Rock method to learn how to become invisible to a narcissist. People with a narcissist tendency feed off the energy of other people, so when we disengage with them, when we don't argue with them or let them get an emotional charge out of us, we are no longer a source for them to feed from. I used to repeat *Gray Rock, Gray Rock,* to myself over and over to remind myself not to engage when in the presence of someone with narcissistic tendencies.

Not engaging when I am emotionally charged is now part of my personal boundaries. The reason I validated Jack's stories to his friends and family about my crazy behavior is because I was physically, mentally, and emotionally exhausted. All the gaslighting had me second-guessing myself. And when he would poke me in public under those conditions, I felt crazy and would lash out, validating his stories of how crazy I was. Now I know if I am tired or emotionally charged not to engage. Period. Trust me, when the ego is going, it is hard to refrain, but when I realized that the cost of validating his story was higher than telling my ego to shut up, it was easier to not play into his hand.

We tell people not to drive cars or operate heavy equipment when under the influence of drugs or alcohol, but we don't have a warning label when we're emotionally charged, distorting our ability to communicate effectively in emotionally charged moments. Having important conversations under the influence of emotionally charged feelings is like driving drunk. Every heightened emotion creates a chemical reaction in the body. Think about this: Have you ever had an experience when you were angry and said something you later wished you could take back? Have you ever been so happy when someone asked you to commit to something, and you agreed to it— only later when you came down off that high to ask yourself why you'd said yes? Or how about when you felt sad? Have you ever just shriveled up and missed out on a great opportunity?

If I am feeling emotionally charged or exhausted while engaged in a conversation, I tell the person that I'm having an emotional reaction or that I'm emotionally charged right now and that I would rather not say something I can't take back. I tell them that I will reconnect with them later, tomorrow, or another time. It is okay to take a breath and a moment to find clarity before you speak; it is called self-love, and again, it is not selfish to make such requests. If someone has a problem with it, I will note that as a red flag and double down on creating space to find my balance and choose from that place.

And since we are on the topic of being off-balance emotionally, mentally, and physically, let's also talk about love-bombing (which I've mentioned I experienced several times). From my journaling, I realized that love-bombing is a red flag. In unhealthy relationships, this is usually introduced right at the beginning of the relationship. It can be anything from multiple text messages in a day, phone calls, or trying to make plans to see you every night. I was flattered initially that someone was so interested in me that they wanted to shower me with all their attention. For this addict, it felt like being at an all-you-can-eat buffet of much-desired attention. Be careful. It is the chef calling you, the frog, into the pot. You will enjoy the attention and maybe even get addicted to it, and when they have you emotionally off-balance and so in love, the switch flips and the awful, abusive behavior replaces the million lovey texts you used to get. You will begin to gaslight yourself, wondering what you did wrong and how to return to the old days. But that is just it. There is no going back; it only gets worse.

If you find yourself in that situation, please be gentle with yourself. Most of us who are people-pleasers have been addicted to some form of unhealthy behavior most of our lives. We tend not to be kind to ourselves when we discover, in hindsight, the red flags of unhealthy relationships we have found ourselves in yet again. We can be so cruel to ourselves during the recovery process we become our *own* abusers with our negative self-talk. With awareness comes the opportunity to make new choices and create healthier outcomes. We did not become people-pleasing addicts overnight, so why do we think we can recover in a moment? It takes time to create new "samskaras" or new habits.

LEARNING WHAT HEALTHY RELATIONSHIPS LOOK LIKE AND HOW TO identify red flags was just the beginning of my road to recovery. During this time my coach Colleen also introduced me to R.C. Blake Jr.'s books *Soul Ties: Breaking the Ties that Bind* and *The Father Daughter Talk*. Both books had a major impact in changing my awareness, thoughts, and beliefs. In *Soul Ties*, Blake talks about how, when we are physically intimate with a person, a "soul tie" between the parties is created. He encourages women to use discernment when it comes to intimacy because our physical, spiritual, and emotional well-being are at risk. One of the ways he encourages us to cut any soul ties is to completely cut off all contact with the other person, which also includes releasing any items received or that remind you of the other person.

I struggled with the thought of releasing Lady G (my motorcycle) and even the two office cabinets I always wanted. I journaled about how I did not want to give those material items up, and at first I was angry that I still had beliefs that without a man I could not have those things. I questioned why I did not feel worthy of abundance and ultimately realized what was playing in the background of my mind were my unconscious beliefs that had been programmed in my early years telling me that I would not have success or financial security without a man.

I did decide to sell, give away, or donate anything that stirred up unhealthy emotions around any and every unhealthy relationship I'd had. I wanted to heal myself, and if giving up a few materialistic items was the way to do that, it seemed a small price to pay. I focused on healing so that I could create my own abundance and security and buy anything I needed or that my heart desired in the future.

In addition to all my above learning, I watched YouTube videos of

Dr. Marissa Peer and learned scripts to use to stand up for myself when I was in conversations with potential predators. I also read books like *Dodging Energy Vampires*, by Dr. Christine Northrop, *Setting Boundaries Will Set You Free* and *Worthy: Boost Your Self Worth to Grow Your Net Worth*, by Nancy Levin, to name a few. I loaded my Kindle, Audible, and podcast lists with everything I could learn from and that would inspire me to keep moving forward into the unknown and away from my addiction or old unhealthy behaviors. I had pangs of withdrawal from Jack, and in the beginning they were frequent, but as the year went on, they would come and go from time to time. I had to remember my "why" for leaving him. My drug of choice—male attention and security—while under its influence had allowed me to create a fairy-tale illusion of what type of guy Jack was and to ignore the reality of who he really was. When I saw him through my rose-tinted glasses—based on my need for safety and security—I saw him as I wanted him to be, not as who he really was: a control freak. I was so in love with being in love I had convinced myself that the unhealthy behaviors our relationship showed early on were because he loved and cared about me. I romanticized his control. He knew the right things to say and do, and I gave him the road map.

R.C. Blake created an awareness that I had been telling Jack and other men what I was looking for by sharing my desires, wins, and wounds on social media platforms. I gave potential harmful partners the road map to my mind, heart, and soul. People who want to control relationships are excellent researchers. What all my predators have in common is that they studied me and what made me tick. Without even realizing it, my social media was giving them intel and insight into how I thought and what I wanted. Jack played into my addiction of my belief that I needed a man because he knew I was in love with the idea of love. I watched *The Bachelor* like a die-hard foot-ball fan watches the Superbowl. That was why very early on in our relationship he would hint about getting engaged. It was bread-crumbing—giving me small bites of what he knew I wanted so I would continue to follow him around like a duck with a piece of bread waiting for the loaf that never comes. For my birthday in

August of 2020, he bought me a mail order "To My Future Wife Letter" fleece throw blanket. And at another time he bought me a Miami Dolphins jersey with his last name on it. He knew how to feed my addiction. I had no idea he was researching my entire Facebook profile, gathering data to use as a drug and feed my addictions.

While I was high on the flattery that someone wanted to know everything about me, I wasn't aware that very often predators will avoid sharing information about themselves, or if they do, they are very aloof about it. That is another red flag to be aware of: when someone does not answer a question but runs circles around it. They want to know everything about you, but it's not because they care (like I often made it mean to me) but because they are looking for your weak spots. Now when I meet someone new, if they immediately ask about my past or former relationships in a first meeting, I will avert the conversation. I use discernment and make sure that the level of sharing is on the same level and that the conversation and sharing is appropriate.

What I did not know was that all my self-work—the reading, classes, and coaching—was about to be tested in a big way. I was house-sitting for my dear friend Angie when I received a call at six a.m. on Friday, September 10, 2021, telling me that my mom had passed away. I retreated to my friend's beautiful patio that I like to call a sanctuary. The view from the patio is a paradise of tall trees, lush gardens that attract beautiful butterflies, bird baths and feeders for various birds and of course the squirrels. I could not be more grateful for such a beautiful space to process the loss of my mother as I journaled my grief. As much as I was mourning the loss of my mother, I was equally uncomfortable with the thought of returning to North Carolina to bury her alongside my dad. I was filled with fear and anxiety over family dynamics and the probability of running into Jack while I was in town. I had to once again pull myself together since I was in the middle of a two-day training for a client.

I called my client that morning and told them the news of my mother's passing. I assured them that I could get through the training to bring us to completion since they had made the arrangements to make staff available after hours. We agreed not to tell the staff of my mom's passing. At first I had no idea how I made it through that training, but now I realize that once again I tapped into my coping mechanism that helped me survive through all the years of trauma. I had learned how to go numb, which served me for that time, but it also robbed me of feeling other emotions and creating deeper bonds with my sons and friends.

When I got home later that day, I still did not have time to process the loss of my mom. I had to go into preparation of her celebration of life and my return into the lion's den. I knew that I was emotionally off-balance, which meant that I was susceptible to making bad choices. I made myself a list of all the reasons I had left Jack, in case I was tempted in my moments of grief to seek comfort in the familiar. I called a few friends and shared the reasons I chose the fork in the road in case my willpower was not enough to stay strong for myself under the circumstances. Some of my friends expressed concern about me going back to North Carolina and being so close to Jack, but I knew the pain he'd caused me, and I also knew I was not going to give him the satisfaction of crawling back to him or to let him hinder my being present for my mom's service. What I told my friends was they *should* be concerned about someone new coming in during this time while I was emotionally off-balance.

Because of some family dynamics at dinner the night we all arrived in North Carolina, I submitted to having a margarita. I knew I was using it as a crutch to help me numb my discomfort and grief. When I walked back to my hotel room across from the restaurant, I could see Jack's store down the road. As I got back to my room, I was feeling sad, lonely, and exhausted. I started to reminisce about my time with Jack. Of course, only the fun memories came back of us cruising along the beach on the motorcycle, dining at our favorite restaurant, etc. I pulled out my list to remind me of the reality of our relationship, and when that still was not enough, I called one of my friends for additional support.

I made it through that evening, and the next day I decided to skip a family outing and spend time with myself. I wanted to protect my fragile state and to keep myself as grounded as possible. I decided to take myself to lunch at my favorite restaurant, seeing as this would be the last time I returned to the area. I was enjoying a lovely meal at the bar when a gentleman interrupted me to comment on my food selection. He was a tall, handsome doctor. He told me I should have ordered the stuffed dates. After a few playful exchanges, the next thing I knew, he was sitting next to me sharing stuffed dates.

We went out on a date a couple of days after my mom's funeral as I was still wrapping up some last things. We shared food, we went for a walk on the beach, and danced in the rain. It was a lovely time. It was a great distraction from my grief and drama, but part of me knew deep down he was the "new" person I had warned my friends about. We kept in touch after my return to Florida, but with all my learning about red flags still so fresh in my mind, even in my time of grief and when I was most vulnerable, I was able to identify them and cut him loose very early. *(Yes, I did it! Please feel free to cheer.)*

The version of myself that had existed before I learned what healthy relationships look like would have entertained the good-looking doctor longer. After all, a doctor would have been able to give me the security I was desperately seeking, right? But I was starting to realize that what I thought was security was only a fairy tale. Growing up with unhealthy relationships all around me had made them my normal. It was not until I started to learn what healthy relationships required, and that it was possible to unlearn the unhealthy relationship patterns I'd grown up with, that I was able to change my behavior and create new, healthier outcomes. In the almost five months after I had returned to Florida, before my mom passed, all my studying, coaching, therapy, and uncomfortable introspection had made all the difference in how my trip to my mom's funeral transpired. My leap of faith was already proving to have been the right choice.

Now it was time to focus on *me* and the life I truly desired.

CHAPTER NINE

EVERY MAN IS MY DAD

When I returned to Florida after my mom's funeral, it was hard to find a new place to call home—it was still during Covid—as well as build up the money for the security deposits and furnishings. Finally, after eight long months of couch-surfing after leaving Jack, I settled in an adorable one-bedroom apartment on the second floor of a historic building smack in the middle of a cute downtown in central Florida.

I wanted my apartment to feel like a hug. A place I could feel safe in and call home. An acquaintance of my coach, Colleen, was an interior designer. She helped me mindfully select and lay out the furniture. She inspired ideas for soft ceiling-to-floor curtains that added warmth to the cathedral ceilings and other decor that created my cozy space.

Now with a place to call home, I could finally breathe and really focus on my recovery and healing journey. Not only was my apartment in a quaint downtown but I was also within walking distance of a beautiful lake where I spent many mornings and hours in contemplation.

One day in February of 2023 after another distasteful hit of my favorite drug—male attention—I was led to a bench that overlooked the lake to ponder what had transpired in that experience. I stopped at my favorite coffee shop to grab what I call a hug-in-a-mug (Lavender Latte) to comfort me as I would once again take a look deep within myself to understand how I keep ending up with the same kind of controlling guy, over and over again.

As I started to take inventory of all the men in my life, and thanks to the CHAT Communication methodology I'd created, I had a huge aha! moment. But before I share this life-changing breakthrough, I must take you back to the beginning—when I first created CHAT—for you to understand how I created it and to have a basic understanding of how the methodology works. Since I first developed CHAT in 2016, I have been refining it over the years and teaching the methodology to organizations, corporations, and individuals through workshops, keynotes, and coaching sessions.

I did not realize how much the creation of CHAT would be one of the biggest tools in my healing tool belt until I started to write this chapter and my editor created awareness that I am indeed writing a memoir and that there would be a delicate balance between my personal story and promoting my company. It was in that moment when I looked over my years of research, teaching, and development that I saw that CHAT had been the vehicle for me to reconnect with my own voice. It gave me a platform to stand on and to help others communicate their authentic voices as well. It not only provided me with an income, but over the years it had helped me pull back the layers of my deeply conditioned beliefs about myself and to freely explore who I really am.

It's been said that we teach what we need to learn the most. When I was developing CHAT, I didn't realize how much my communication research and facilitation with others would continue to heal me at this point in my journey.

As you know by now, growing up I didn't feel valued, seen, or heard. So as a part of my healing journey, I became obsessed with human behavior. I studied every personality tool and consumed as

many books as possible to understand my experiences. I quickly realized that, although those tools helped me learn a lot about myself, I
didn't know much about how to communicate with others in my life.
Learning about many tools often took a lot of time for me to understand and apply the knowledge. Sometimes the resources left me
more confused than when I started. That was when it hit me! I saw an
opportunity to simplify the information I was learning to be more
digestible and to help us understand each other's preferred communication styles.

Most of personality-assessment science is based on the same
theories, flavored with the creator's own twist. I decided to reverse-
engineer the process. I was so excited I immediately created spread-
sheets and made Post-it notes to stick to the walls of my office under
each communication style I was creating. I started to group certain
communication behaviors together and saw commonality within four
distinct communication styles.

Then I wanted to figure out what to call my process, so I looked at
using different words and then looked up their meaning to see if they
had the meaning that resonated with what I was trying to convey. I
first looked up "talk," defined as "speak to give information." Then I
looked up the word "chat," and its definition was "Talk in a friendly
and casual way." Chat felt more like what I was creating: a way for us
to speak to each other in a friendly and casual way so we are open
enough to hear new ideas, thoughts, etc.

I then started to look for words that would encompass each of the
four styles I had identified. The catch was that they had to make
sense and still spell *chat*.

Using a dictionary and thesaurus, plus Google, I came up with a
memorable acronym that also reflected communication! CHAT
stands for Creative, Harmony, Action, and Template communication
styles. Below I share a brief description of each style and the types of
people most associated with each.

Creative communication style: "out of the box" thinkers who tend
to be more introverted. They often enjoy their own company and feel
exhausted by small talk. They believe every problem has a solution

and ask a lot of "Why?" questions. Often their forward-thinking solutions can be perceived by those with other three styles as crazy. Creatives like to do their own research and make their own decisions in their own time. Trying to force the Creatives to make a decision is like trying to put a cat in a bubble bath. If you try to force an outcome, they will lash out and not in the way you had hoped.

Harmony communication style: people who want us to get along and form a fair society for all. They avoid conflict at any cost and say yes when they probably really want to say no to avoid disappointing people. When they listen to others speak, they can often relate with great empathy. A Harmony needs to feel connection with the individuals they are speaking with and that everyone is being treated fairly. They are the busy bees in our networks, communities, and families. They know a lot of people and are always looking to connect others who have what each person needs.

Action communication style: often shocks others with what they say and are very passionate. They are the movers and shakers, and their passion can be perceived as being aggressive. They like to approach situations with the attitude of *Let's throw spaghetti at the wall and see what sticks*. They dislike speaking with people who do not get straight to the point.

Template communication style: prefers the correct use of grammar, and they value credentials. They work best from a to-do list, and any unexpected changes to their agenda throw them off track. The Templates are the rule followers. They prefer to see things in black and white. They feel most comfortable with a predictable, controlled environment.

It's likely you resonated with more than one style because everyone has all four communication styles within them already. We all have what I like to call a primary and secondary style that we are most comfortable with. They are where we spend most of our time. We tend to surround ourselves with people with similar primary and secondary communication styles without realizing it because it feels easy; they just get us. Our third communication style can move into second place or last place. For example, if your first three communication styles are Template, Harmony, and Action, you sometimes would be inspired to make things happen, and other days you might just want to sit on the couch and eat bonbons.

Our last one is what I call our biggest opportunity. It is our least favorite and we try to avoid it like many of us try to avoid going to the dentist. Have you ever walked into a networking event or party and there is someone you just want to avoid at all costs because you don't like talking with them? Chances are their primary is your opportunity. It isn't even personal. You just do not like to use that communication style, which is why I call it an opportunity.

When we cut someone off because they happen to lead with our own opportunity we cut into our potential partnerships, next job opportunities, or even a new friend by twenty-five percent! In business, that is leaving a lot on the table. The more off-balance we are between our styles, the higher that percentage goes. Let's say you only prefer to surround yourself with your primary and secondary communication styles, then that percentage would go up to fifty!

The idea of CHAT is to learn how to come in and out of the four CHAT styles to create solutions and work together when needed. Have you heard of the Golden Rule? Do unto others as you would have done unto yourself. That does not always work in communication; you have only a twenty-five percent chance of speaking to someone outside your inner circle who leads with your preferred style. If you love all the details and talk to someone who wants to get straight to the point, they might nod their head in agreement as you talk, but most likely they are not listening and are thinking to themselves about how they want you to stop talking. The Platinum Rule comes in here: speak to others how they like to be spoken to. I did not create CHAT to be used as a manipulation tool. It also was not created to fake relationships. It was created so we can easily and quickly identify different communication styles and meet someone where they are so we can move closer to creating peace in our society —one conversation at a time.

When I first created CHAT, I thought my communication style was Harmony, Creative, Action, and Template (HCAT). I used to end my CHAT training or keynotes by saying that "CHAT was created by a Harmony for harmony." As I deepened my research and continued to refine the methodology, I discovered that I was only HCAT because of my childhood conditioning and people-pleasing tendencies. As I explored my true essence over the years, I realized I was the original acronym! I was CHAT! If you are curious to know what your CHAT Communication Style is, please see the complimentary CHAT assessment at the end of this book.

As you've read, I had been conditioned my whole life to not rock the boat. I spent most of my life feeling like I was walking on eggshells to please a man. I tried my best to avoid conflict at all costs, which led me to follow in my mom's footsteps of being a people-pleaser and saying yes when it should have been no. As I did my own personal growth research and inner work, I realized that being a people-pleaser was not being true to my authentic self. I started to study more about creating boundaries and how to say no while holding my ground. This allowed me to embrace my true communication style.

People are often shocked when they learn that I am not Action or Harmony first. The version they see of me on the stage is my work self. I am silly and outgoing. I do this to fulfill my life purpose. It is practicing what I preach about coming in and out of the four styles as needed to get the goal or vision accomplished. But afterward, I need my own space to recharge my batteries. Often after a speaking engagement I will block three days off to recover because my natural communication style is more introverted.

NOW THAT YOU HAVE THE BASIC KNOWLEDGE OF CHAT AND HOW THE methodology works, let's go back to what had brought me to that day in February 2023 when I was sitting in the park, sipping my hug-in-a-mug and contemplating how I kept getting the same results with the men I dated. About a month prior, I had decided that I had done enough self-work after leaving Jack to start testing my new knowledge. And, well... to be honest, my addiction told me I needed some male attention. So I thought it would be a good idea to join a dating site. I met a guy named Steven and we had similar interests, both rode motorcycles, enjoyed ballroom dancing, and we each were self-proclaimed foodies. He was good-looking but not really my type, looks wise. He was originally from Greece and spoke with an accent, which often led to misunderstandings in language and culture. I gave him several passes on some "off" remarks he made, but after our final round of texts about who was breaking up with whom—need I mention he was a complete control freak?—I ended the relationship.

While sitting on the bench, I went through each man and relationship I'd had, and I started to use my CHAT system to assess their communication styles. With each person, I started to notice a pattern: each one had my dad's communication style! Wow, my mind was blown away. Years ago, during one of my earlier CHAT workshops, I had a young woman stand up and ask me why she repeatedly attracted men who had the opposite of her communication style. My response was that we attract what we lack. She then asked how she could stop doing that. I told her to become more balanced in all four communication styles and then she would no longer attract that type of partner. I had no idea that I had been literally speaking and teaching *exactly* what I would need to hear all these years later.

That discovery was fascinating to me. I have witnessed people come into a CHAT training and then see them six months later, and they ask me if it is possible that their communication style could have changed. Yes, it is possible to change your communication style. Unlike some other personality assessments, CHAT was designed knowing that our communication style is based on our conditioning, experiences, education, etc. That means with time, understanding, and a willingness to learn, we can peel back the layers of our conditioning and discover who we really are. It was never meant to pigeonhole people into certain categories. It was designed to be a tool to help us communicate more effectively and to be more fluid.

I always tell people that CHAT has many applications and unlimited possibilities because it does! Chances are you may notice a similarity in your relationships. Not only did creating the CHAT methodology help me pull back my own layers and get to know myself but it also showed me the pattern or cycle of my own relationships.

Mentally going through the communication styles of every relationship I have ever had, I realized *I had been chasing my lost relationship with my dad for years. For my entire life I was trying to win back the love I had longed for.*

I had created the same childhood scenario over and over again. With my dad being primarily an ATCH style, he was not easily impressed. I felt like I could never live up to his expectations of me, and I ultimately found and dated men with similar styles to keep me on the treadmill of trying to prove myself and win their attention and affection that I so deeply desired. Because I was an HCAT communication style, the people-pleaser in me wanted that male stamp of approval and deeply craved love and affection. I can remember sharing a college report card with my dad. I had achieved a 4.0 GPA and even made the dean's list. I thought I finally had done it: I would impress my dad and win his love and affection. But in a split-second my hope turned into despair when he said, "That is all you did? What about an A+?" The wind was knocked out of my soul. With Action his primary style, he was very competitive by nature and, as a Template secondary, believed in tough love and that there was always room for improvement. I now realize that for him, this was his way of showing support, but for my Harmony heart back then, it lacked everything I needed to truly thrive. Harmony communication styles crave words of affirmation and affection. I was like a dog who retrieves a ball, waiting for the pat on the head. My need for approval was so deeply ingrained in me I was repeating the cycle with every man, and every time, my relationships ended the same way, with me struggling with my self-esteem and feeling unworthy. Which further reinforced my childhood stories of me not being enough. It is powerful to have this realization, and even as I write this, I have tears. Throughout my life I had taken the unconscious beliefs that were running in the back of my mind and brought them into my conscious thoughts. The exciting part was that now that I was aware of unconscious beliefs and patterns, I could consciously change them.

Not only had I been attracting my dad's communication style in my romantic relationships, but it also turned out that his primary and secondary communication styles were what I was lacking. The advice I shared years ago with the woman from my training was exactly what I needed to hear to heal myself. With my dad being an ATCH (Action, Template, Creative, Harmony) and me being a CHAT (Creative, Harmony, Action, Template), his primary and secondary were my opportunities and vice versa. My dad's opportunity (Harmony) was my primary—before I realized my true nature—and I craved for him to be more supportive and loving. Because my dad was an ATCH, he would often shock people, had a tight wallet (unless he chose not to), and sometimes he could see the big picture and other times not; Harmony, his "opportunity," meant that he was not very affectionate or sensitive.

It's likely my dad's communication style was formed from his own childhood and conditioning. I believe because after my "uncomfortable conversation" with him (Chapter 4), he became childlike in our conversations and wanted to connect more. Maybe, deep down, Harmony was higher than his last communication style. I will never know, but I do know that it is not too late for me to embrace my own opportunity communication style, Template, and engage my discernment more as I move forward in life.

Because of this life-changing aha! moment, I was ready to further prioritize me and take my boundaries and healing to a whole new level of liberation. My exhilarating journey of creating the life I've always dreamed of had begun.

CHAPTER TEN

THE EDGE OF FREEDOM

Throughout my journey to recovering and prioritizing myself, I had picked the resources and tools based on what I was trying to overcome or accomplish. I used therapy to work through my rape and other traumas, and I used coaches to learn new tools to move forward. After my aha! moment about how I had chosen men similar to my father, I started to notice how busy my mind was and how the voice in my head seemed to never turn off. I wanted peace and quiet! Over the years, I have dabbled with yoga, but I have never stuck with it long enough to make it a practice. I decided it was time to give it another try.

I became like Goldilocks from the *The Three Bears*—trying on yoga studios near my home until I found my "just right" place. The style of yoga that worked for me was restorative yoga. Restorative yoga holds each pose longer than regular asana-style yoga, sometimes holding each pose for between three to five minutes, allowing the body to sink deeply into each pose. It helped me really slow down all the thoughts in my mind and just relax. Because my mind was quiet, I was able to have many breakthroughs. I would get insights into healing past trauma and answers to things I would later write about in my journals just to get them out of my head. After class, I would share them with my teachers.

In April 2023, one of my teachers suggested that I consider taking yoga teacher training, but I laughed him off as I walked out the door. I never thought about it again until months later, when sharing another insight after class, the instructor's wife asked me if I'd ever thought about attending teacher training. I looked at her and asked if they were working together to recruit people for the training. She looked surprised. She had no idea that her husband had offered me the training months prior. I then asked her why I should consider teacher training. Her response was profound. She asked, "Wouldn't it be nice to give back to a practice that has given you so much?" Ouch, she got me! That rang as truth through my whole body.

In my next session with my new Human Design coach, Charllotte, I shared my experience of being invited (which is correct for my design) to take the training and all the reasons my ego had against it. Like the cost of the program, how I didn't see myself teaching classes in a studio, did I want to give up every other weekend for six months, and on and on. Then Charllotte asked me one question: "Can you do it just for the experience, not knowing the outcome?"

Charllotte always has a way of saying something profound to me and then allowing me to have my time and space to process and wait for my emotional clarity. It took me a few months to reach my place of neutral to hear my "yes" to commit to the yoga teaching program. After months of waiting, I showed up to the very first day of teacher training completely nervous and not knowing what to expect.

In yoga, there is a saying about being at "the edge" of a pose and learning how to breathe into it. This is the point where you feel different sensations in different parts of your body as you sink into poses, and it burns but not to where it is painful. The idea is to focus on your breath and follow "the edge" as it moves from location to location. You can feel a pulling of your muscles or tightness; for some, it is tingling. The burn can sometimes make you want to release the pose, but if you breathe through it, the body will release the trapped energy on its own when you relax into it. One day, we were taking a rope wall class. A rope wall class is exactly that: a wall that has different heights and types of ropes coming off it to assist the student in obtaining the most out of a pose while being supported by the ropes. One time, I had the ropes around my waist, and I was bending over forward. I could feel my edge—it came hard and quick—and I was embracing my breath to help me push past my edge. I made it to the end of the pose, and as soon as I got off the wall, I sobbed uncontrollably. It was straight-up ugly crying with my nose running, gasping for air in between my tears. One of the yoga teachers took me to the waiting area and gently held space for me to feel every emotion that was coming up to be healed.

It is believed that emotions that are not fully processed (for example, when we cry but stop because we are told not to cry in public) are stored in the body unprocessed. In the book *Untethered Soul* by Michael Singer, he talks about how we are meant to feel emotions or have experiences and to let them go through us. It is when we stop the process of having those thoughts or emotions that they then get stored in the body and later show up as "dis-ease." I have no idea what that huge emotion of release was. Of course, my ego wanted to label it, make it about something specific, but there really was no rhyme or reason for it. It was a huge purge of emotions that had been trapped in my body for who knows how long.

Once I got over my initial embarrassment of being the first one to have an emotional release during our teacher training, I did notice a sense of peace and "room" in my body. I was fascinated with the theory and principles behind yoga. I had always thought yoga was fancy poses done by skinny people who look Instagram fabulous, but the truth is that yoga is now my lifestyle. During teacher training, we learned about the history of yoga, the body's anatomy, the eight limbs of yoga, and not just asana, which is physical practice, but about other limbs of yoga, breathing, mudras, and mastering the mind. My favorite book we read was *Yamas & Niyamas* by Deborah Adele. I use the principles in that book as my guide for living my day-to-day life. I also believe that adopting those principles paved the way for more deep emotional release, which led me to my next transformative experience.

One day we were practicing restorative yoga, my favorite. As I mentioned, restorative yoga is a slower form of yoga than asana. I loved to use props such as bolsters, blankets, or blocks to assist me in poses. As I was holding a pose and feeling supported by the props, I was finally able to drop fully into the pose. I will never forget that moment because it was the first time I felt supported by the universe. It was a beautiful and intimate dance between me and the divine. That was when I realized that I was not alone and that the universe does have my back. It was the first time I can remember feeling safe. I cannot fully express in words what happened in that moment, but it changed my dance with the divine and more importantly how I interacted with myself. It was a profound feeling of deep love and peace. It was the love/feeling I had been searching for my whole life, not just from men but from my mother, my siblings, and mates. It was so beautiful. Throughout my life I had always felt alone and abandoned, but it was in that moment, in the quiet, in the surrender, that I realized I was never alone. But my ego and all its noise had me distracted from my connection to source, Divine, Love, Universe, God.

AN AMAZING OPPORTUNITY CAME UP FOR ME TO BUY AN RV IN A NEARBY central Florida community. As you know, I have always had the dream to travel. I would see pictures of places from around the globe, and my eyes would fill up from the beauty I had yet to discover. I have always dreamed of traveling to beautiful locations to immerse myself in different cultures, dancing, and people. I loved my cozy apartment, but it made sense to me to have an RV as a home base to lower my monthly expenses so I could live large and travel the world.

Colleen, my first Human Design coach, told me about a possible opportunity to buy an RV in a park near her home. I went to see it, and while it was an older RV, it had a lot of potential. The man whom it belonged to had passed away, and his son was selling the RV. I made him an offer on it with two conditions. Since the park was a "fifty-five and over" community and I was not fifty-five yet, management would approve me to live in the park and that the RV could stay on the lot it was on, which backed up to the national forest.

I made the offer on a Sunday, so that Monday morning, I had to go back and fill out the application to see if I would be approved. While I was waiting for my application results, I also needed to come up with a solution for getting out of my apartment's lease. I texted two people who I knew were looking for places to live. I explained my situation and asked them if they would be interested in taking over my lease if my landlord agreed. Within minutes they both said yes! Shortly after receiving those text messages, I got a call from the RV park office. I had been approved. Next it was time to reach out to my landlord. I told her that I had an amazing opportunity to buy an RV and finally make my dreams of travel come true! I also told her that I had found two different people to take over my lease if she was interested in meeting them and that I would stay until the end of May. My landlord told me that she appreciated me finding people to take over my lease but that it was not necessary. She would let me out of my lease with no penalties and wished me well on my new adventure.

I love how when we confidently step into our dreams the universe lines up and creates magic. Not only did I manage to manifest two people to take over my lease within minutes, I got approved for the RV park in a few minutes, my landlord let me out of my lease with no penalties, and if that was not enough evidence, the universe even lined up that the new tenants would buy almost all my furniture so I didn't have to deal with selling it on Facebook or moving it. Talk about magic!

Over the next month and a half, when I was not working or in yoga teacher training, I spent every free second renovating the RV, as I wanted to finish it before moving in on June 1. I hired someone to clean the place, but they did not clean it to my standards. As I was cleaning the RV from ceiling to floor, I started to feel overwhelmed with the extent of the project. I had bleach water falling on me from the ceiling when Colleen came over to talk with me. She noticed I was irritated and tried to remind me why I bought "Freedom," which was what I named the RV because she was supposed to help me keep my monthly bills low so I would have the freedom to travel. As Colleen tried to remind me of this, I told her, "Fuck Freedom." I was ready to give up on my dream, but once I calmed down, I was ready to keep moving forward.

Over the next few weeks, I did things I thought I would never be able to do. With the support of Colleen, her knowledge of do-it-yourself projects, and YouTube university, I was pulling up carpets, laying tile, using power tools, fixing plumbing, and even climbing up on the roof of the RV to do roof repairs; and my dear friend Regina taught me how to paint all the cabinets! Freedom was a labor of love and hope. I was extremely impressed with myself and how much I could do, which was more than I ever thought I was capable of. I was feeling accomplished when I moved in that June. The RV was completely renovated, and anyone who saw the before-and-after pictures could not believe the drastic makeover.

With the fresh coat of paint, curtains, and throw pillows, it was darling at first. As time went on, the two-hour round trips back and forth to yoga teacher training on top of already long days started to take a physical toll on me. Then, even though I'd had someone look over the RV prior to buying it—and I was told it was in great shape and a steal of a deal—it turned out that it needed some more work. First it was the brand-new toilet I put in that I later found out had a recall because it gave off horrific smells even after cleaning the tanks that needed replaced. Then the AC was not working correctly. I had to install a new refrigerator, and the roof needed to be sealed. It seemed like it was one thing after another and my dream to have minimum living expenses so I could travel was quickly starting to fade.

And if *that* was not enough to make me regret my decision, I could not enjoy my swing outside because I lived so close to the national forest. I could not use any type of bug spray! The moment I set foot out my RV, I was eaten alive by mosquitoes and horseflies. One night while cooking a beautiful salmon dinner for Colleen to thank her for help with the RV, out of nowhere I started to notice one fly, then a few more, and within moments, there were hundreds of flies inside my RV. The next day, I looked for every possible entrance and sealed them all. It appeared to do the trick until the next time, when I had my friend Ashley over for dinner and I again made salmon. Within seconds, hundreds of flies invaded again. I was mortified and livid at the same time.

But that was only the beginning of my bug issues. It was the rainy season, and with the amount of rain that we were having in the forest, every bug also wanted to be dry and warm. My RV quickly became a place for cockroaches to seek refuge from the rain. One day, I was putting on my shirt when I realized that one was inside it! I screamed like I had just witnessed a murder. I dislike bugs of any kind but especially roaches. With the help of a fellow yoga student, I found a natural bug repellent and gave my RV a healthy dose of it, but it didn't help much, and I was having a difficult time sleeping knowing that there were bugs roaming around while I was trying to sleep. I was sharing my fear of sleeping with bugs with my yoga teacher, and she brought a profound insight to me. She said that the roaches in the nighttime were a symbol of unconsented touch. Wow, that was it. That was why I felt so violated and did not want to sleep, much less live, in the RV anymore.

I was at my edge! Between all the driving back and forth, being stuck in a small RV, the constant financial demands, and lack of sleep were all getting to me. And it had only been two months of living in the RV. I was on a call with my friend Tracey, telling her all my challenges and how defeated I felt. She said, "Do you remember what you told me at the beginning of this adventure when I questioned your decision? You told me that if this did not work out, you could sell the RV and do something different." Holy cow! It was a clear example that the universe had my back again. I had completely forgotten that I said that, and in my time of need, I happened to be talking to the right person to remind me. I never felt so relieved; it was as if I could breathe again! I decided to sell Freedom.

In early July, I'd had a coaching session with Megha, who used palm prints to assist her in her coaching methods. During our session, I was sitting in my RV. She told me that when she viewed my website and saw my photos and materials, that there was a disconnect between who I am now and who I want to be. She asked me why I lived in an RV. I explained to her that I was trying to live small financially so I could live large and travel. Megha then told me that according to my Human Design, I am meant to be bougie (bourgeoisie) and asked why I was ashamed or afraid to own that part of myself. She then went on to ask me why I felt the need to play small. This was a huge moment for me, and I needed time to explore those important questions.

A few days later, Tracey's partner, Pat, called me and asked me what my plans were now that I'd decided to sell my RV. She told me about an amazing studio apartment near them in South Florida, just off the beach, that a friend of hers had for rent. I already had a trip planned to stay at Tracey and Pat's condo for my birthday (to get some peace away from my RV), so I arranged to see the apartment while I was in town. I drove past the apartment at different times of the day and week. When I finally got to see it, my gut knew it was for me. After viewing it, I went out for coffee with my potential new landlord. When I told her that I would not be able to take the apartment until October because of upcoming travel plans and completing my yoga teacher training, she agreed to hold the apartment for me!

I immediately went into fear after I agreed to take the apartment by the beach. I had only been paying a couple hundred dollars a month for the RV lot rental, and now I was looking at close to two thousand dollars a month in expenses, not to mention that all my insurance costs would also be going up. When talking with Colleen, she also expressed concerns about my additional expenses but mostly because she loves to be very thrifty herself. I reviewed my coaching session with Megha and asked myself, Why do I live so limited? And why had I been denying my bougie desires? Do I not trust that the universe would rise to meet me and my desires?

So, even with my fears, I decided to go for it. I told my potential new landlord that I wanted to sell my RV before signing the lease.

She agreed to hold the apartment. I still had some finishing touches on the RV to take care of before I could take pictures and put it up for sale. Since I had an upcoming trip to New York to attend the Omega Leadership Women's Academy during the second week of September, I decided I wanted to be fully present and to hold off on listing the RV for sale until I returned. I figured it would minimize my interruptions and frustrations for not only me but also for potential buyers wanting to come see it.

The day I was traveling home, my new potential landlord wanted to know if I had sold the RV yet, so I told her that I was traveling and was planning on selling it as soon as I got back. She said she would not be able to hold the apartment any longer and would only hold it until September 20, which ironically was my dad's birthday. That only gave me a few days to sell the RV, but I moved forward with listing it for sale. It had some interest, but I felt disappointed when the first few people were no-shows. So when the twentieth approached, I told her I had not sold it but I did have someone coming from Miami to look at it that Friday. She said, "Well, if they are coming all the way from Miami to see it, they must be serious, and I will hold it one more day."

Friday came and went without anyone coming to look at the RV, so I had to call her and let her know. She told me that she was sorry but couldn't hold the apartment any longer. When I told Pat and Tracey that I was not moving, they were as devasted as I was. They even offered to float me the money to secure the apartment until the RV sold, but I turned down the generous offer because I didn't want to have expenses for both places. I was too caught up in fear to see the universe was giving me a solution.

Over the weekend, I had no hits on the RV. I went deeper and deeper into a depression, wondering why the universe cleared the path and aligned everything for this experience only to feel stuck living in a place I now despised. That Monday, after I told my land-lord I could not take the beach apartment, I had two different couples come look at the RV. Since Colleen knew more about RVs than I did, she offered to help me sell it. The first guy was rude and was very disrespectful to his female partner. I told Colleen that I did not care if he offered me above my asking price, I would not sell it to him. Then the next couple came. They were kind and had small children. They were looking for an RV to create memories together. They were interested but wanted to think it over. I told them, "Of course," and I did let them know I had other people interested in it as well.

Later that afternoon they called with an offer, and after some negotiating, we came to an agreement. They were going to give me a deposit the next day, and we would close the deal on that Friday so they could take it before the first of October. Oh my goodness, it hit me that I needed to be out in less than five days! So I loaded my car up with what was in storage into the RV and headed to my best friend Shelly's house to store them. On my drive to Shelly's, I was talking to myself. "Okay, so now what?" Then I remembered what my potential South Florida landlord had said at the end of our last call—that if anything changed to call her. My ego put up such a fight. "Do not call her; she already rented the place. Remember, she had someone waiting on it." Then I asked myself why would I not call her? The worst-case scenario would be what we already knew: she had rented it. So I sent her a text, and within minutes my phone rang! It was her; she said she couldn't believe it. The person who was going to take the apartment disappeared, they had ghosted her, and she had just sat down to list the apartment on MLS. I told her that my RV sale was not official, that I wanted to see if they did show up with the deposit the next day. She agreed to wait again.

The next day, I did sign an agreement and take a deposit, which then led me to give my landlord a deposit and pay for and complete my background check. We agreed that I would move into my apartment in mid-October, after my next trip and my graduation from yoga teacher training. I was soon all moved out of the RV, and we closed on the RV at the local DMV. The two weeks between selling the RV and moving to South Florida were a whirlwind. I stayed with a girlfriend, then I stayed at my friend Angie's house again. Her place is a sanctuary and was perfect for studying for my yoga teacher exams.

Yoga teacher training was one of the most challenging things I have ever accomplished and was also the most rewarding. Not only did it give me a new way to live my life but it also moved trapped emotions and created space; it gave me a deeper connection to myself and the divine, and it even enhanced my abilities as a facilitator. I was able to bring my lessons learned, have more compassion, and be able to hold greater space for those I had the honor to work with. I now even incorporate breathing and yoga poses into my all-day trainings, workshops, and strategic-planning sessions.

Right after completing my yoga teacher training exams and graduation, my sons and friends took me out to dinner to celebrate my accomplishment and my upcoming move to South Florida. The next day, I would be leaving early with my dear friend Robin to head to Atlanta, Georgia, to attend the TED women's conference for the week. We had a great time at the TED event and headed home on a Friday night. The very next morning I got up at six to pick up the U-Haul and head to Shelly's house for my belongings and then to my new apartment in South Florida!

I arrived late Saturday, and by the time the trailer was unloaded and returned to U-Haul, I was exhausted. The next morning, I decided to take a walk to the beach. When I arrived at the beach opening, it had beautiful palm trees on each side of the path to the ocean. When I looked out and saw the sand and the ocean between the palm trees, I broke down in tears of joy. It was one of the most beautiful things I had ever seen. It took my breath away.

It was in that moment that I realized I had made another lifelong dream come true. I always wanted to live by the beach and here I was. It was now my reality. Then it hit me. Just like how the universe aligned everything for me to have the RV experience that I had desired, it also aligned to create this very moment. All had been in perfect order even when I thought it was not. There is a joke that goes something along the line of, there was a person on a roof and the flood was rising. They were praying to God for help when the helicopter came, and they said, "No, thanks, I am waiting for a sign from God." There were two or three more offers to help, but the person in peril kept refusing. So when they died and got to heaven, they asked God why they did not help, and God's reply was, "I sent you a helicopter."

I tell this because when Tracey and Pat generously offered to front me the money, it was like God sending the helicopter, but I let fear cloud my awareness. The person who ghosted my landlord, which then made my apartment available for me, in my opinion was not a coincidence. I now believe that what is meant for us and is in alignment with our highest purpose cannot be denied.

I now also realize that my anger with the universe for clearing a path to the RV purchase was for my own good. It was something I wanted to experience, so the divine gave me that opportunity. It brought clarity. I can now mark the RV box off, confidently knowing that lifestyle is *not* for me. Had I not had that experience, I would always wonder, and wonder takes up a lot of important real estate in our minds. Now I knew it was time for me to have another much-desired experience of living by the beach and leaning into the divine to create the resources needed to fully live the bougie lifestyle I desired. Freely and without guilt!

I was ready for a rebirth.

CHAPTER ELEVEN

REBIRTH

In Chapter Three, I shared how my eldest son's father did not want my maiden name to be hyphenated on our son's birth certificate. Since I was a single mom, every time I took my son to a doctor's appointment, they would assume my last name was the same as his dad's and call me "Mrs. His Last Name." It was emotionally painful to me, and it felt like someone was rubbing salt into an open wound. When I later got divorced from my second child's father, I wanted to make sure I didn't have that experience again, so I kept my married last name.

Fast forward to the present. I'm living by the beach, my youngest son is in his early twenties with a serious girlfriend, and my ex-husband has had a baby with another woman. It was time to release my married last name. I spoke to each of my sons individually about changing my name. They were both very supportive. After those conversations and during a coaching session, I had clarity and decided to release my married name. I planned to stick with my first and middle names as my middle name was my mother's. Professionally, I have been using Claudia Jean, to pay tribute to my mother and to create a voice to empower myself and other women seeking to speak their truth. Since people in my work life already often used Jean as my last name instead of calling me Claudia Jean, why not make it official? Then my coach said, "Well, since you have clarity about changing your name, would you like to run a numerology report on the name you are considering?"

I am very open-minded about methods that are spiritual or what some call "woo woo" in nature, so, of course, my curiosity kicked in and I said yes. There is a saying about being careful when you open Pandora's box. I had no idea how much my mind would be blown and how much my world would change. Before taking the assessment, I thought of it like any other until I got the results.

The numerology report, based on Kabalistic beliefs, requires your date, time, and location at birth because it is based on astrology to determine your "birth path." It then asks you to provide your birth name, any nicknames, and potential names you may want to use. In Kabalistic philosophy, our names create our personality. Every letter in the alphabet has a number assigned to it. When we take our names and apply numerology, our names translate into numbers. In this assessment, if the name you are using or considering using is not the same as your "birth path" number, you can encounter less pleasant experiences or challenges when trying to fulfill your life's purpose.

I was shocked when I got my results. Everything the report said about my life's purpose was true to my soul. Then it showed everything I was experiencing or would experience using my birth name, nickname, or the name I was considering; it was also bone-chillingly accurate. The report shook me to the core. It talked about how I cannot stand to see another person suffer and that I give more than I receive, which leads to a life full of not only financial struggles but emotional pain. That I would constantly lose what I loved most in life and continue to experience tragedy. My current names would attract more stressful emotional experiences and the tension could impact my entire nervous system. Also, my current names would hinder me from accomplishing my life's purpose.

From still feeling the loss from my early separation from my oldest son to being assaulted by a colleague in my own home and all the other experiences in between, I had all the evidence I needed to validate what the report told me. I read the report several times; I sat with each emotion as it came up. I thought, if I believe everything is vibration and I could accomplish my life purpose just by changing my name, why wouldn't I at least get curious about changing it?

Growing up, I didn't like my name. Claudia was considered an old-fashioned name, and it wasn't common. I remember visiting places like Disney World and looking for my name on a bicycle license plate. Even as an adult, I would look in every gift shop in the hope of finding that my birth name, Claudia, finally made it, and every time, I would feel disappointed when it wasn't there. Months before I decided to release my married name, I went into a candy store, and when I saw the rack of bicycle license plates, I could not help but look. Finally there it was, my name on a license plate! Of course I bought it, but I quickly realized it didn't make me love my name any more.

Because I was not attached to my name and had a willingness to experiment with the universe, I hired a name coach; yes, there is such a thing. The name coach takes your "birth path" number and, using numerology, offers several balanced names that would align with your personality and purpose. I had several hundred first, middle, and last names to consider. They encourage you to read each name out loud, to review the list over several weeks, to read it at different times of the day, and to have a friend read it to you. I took this seriously and I would eliminate names, dwindling them down. I even, at one point, requested more names to consider. I didn't share the list with friends or my coaches. I wanted no outside voices. This decision would be mine and only mine.

Once I got my first name choices down to seven, my middle name down to three choices, and my last name down to five, I then researched each name to see its meaning and origin. Growing up, I didn't know what my heritage was. My mom was adopted, so I only knew about my dad's side. Everyone assumed I was Latin because my birth name was Claudia and I had olive skin. My mom was misinformed by her birth family, who claimed they were Native American. I grew up craving to fit in somewhere, so after taking a DNA test on a bet, I found out that what I thought to know as my truth couldn't be further away from it. I had no Native American ancestry and wasn't Latin. I was disappointed to find out I was whiter than white. If I was going to re-create myself, I wanted to do it in a way that aligned my name with my purpose and my heritage.

I met with my name coach again. We reviewed each of my choices together and narrowed them down even further. She encouraged me to try on my potential new names by asking close friends to call me by it. I went to new places and introduced myself as my possible new name. I observed how I felt and how others interacted with me.

Once I decided on my chosen name, I had another one-to-one conversation with my sons. For those of you wondering, no, I didn't need their permission, but I did promise the boys a long time ago when I realized how my addiction to men impacted my decisions, which in turn created consequences for them, that I would always be transparent in anything that could cause harm to them from that point on. Johnny told me he understood my reasoning and didn't blame me for wanting to change my name. Oliver could understand why I wanted to drop my original names, but being a bit more senti-mental, said, "But Grandma (my mother) selected that name for you." Wow, I never considered that, and it gave me something else to consider. My sons agreed that no matter my legal name, I would always be Mom to them.

I never had thought of asking my mom why she had named me Claudia Jean. I did contemplate that for a while, but then it didn't matter. With everything I had been through up to that point of my life, and what my mom had been through, why would I want to keep the names of such pain, trauma, and loss? If my mom were alive today, what might she say to me if she knew I was considering this change? I believe my mom would have been fully supportive and would have told me to go for it.

The timing to make this type of life change was ideal. I had just moved to South Florida, and only a few old friends knew me there.

They are the same people I asked to explore my new name with me before I ultimately took the necessary steps to change it legally. Most of my inner circle was supportive, and we all did our best to address me by my preferred name. After all, they had known me as Claudia for decades. I didn't get upset when someone accidentally called me by my old name; heck, I was still trying to remember it! I remember in the early weeks of trying on my name, going to the nail salon and checking in as Lorilyn. When I checked out, the person at the register had asked me my name, and without thinking, I had blurted out Claudia. Confused, she looked up at me and said they didn't have a Claudia checked-in! I turned a million shades of red with embarrassment. I quickly said, "Oh, I used my preferred name, Lorilyn." As soon as I got in my car, I laughed so hard! I had forgotten my own name. I shared this story with my friends. Then we started to joke about us going on vacation and them shouting my new name to get my attention and me just walking along, not even recognizing it.

As long as there was effort to respect my choices, I wasn't upset. A few people pushed back, but I have learned that their issues/concerns had nothing to do with me. It was either their belief systems and I was pushing them past their comfort level, or they had their own experiences with something similar and projected them onto my situation.

In January, I decided to go public with my name change and announced it in my newsletter "New Year, New Me!" There was an increase in people who unsubscribed. I also had potential clients questioning why I changed my name. They straight out asked me if I changed my name due to legal issues or unprofessional conduct. Some people may consider my name change drastic or unnecessary. In our society, we do things all the time to change ourselves. We color our hair, wear makeup, and undergo surgeries to enhance our bodies or to lose weight. We go to therapy seeking solutions to life experiences. We hire coaches to support us in reaching our goals. All this in an attempt to better ourselves, so why is a name change difficult for some people to accept? After all, in the Bible, Jesus changed people's names, and when you get married or divorced, you change your name; actors, actresses, authors, etc., do it all the time, and we think nothing about it. It is uncommon for ordinary people, so it gets categorized as drastic, weird, or crazy. We often use those labels when something is outside our comfort zone—to create distance between our beliefs and what is pressing against them and making us uncomfortable—to justify our beliefs to stay comfortable.

During the name-change process, I moved slowly on purpose. I tried on my new name for a few months to ensure I loved it. If I was going to go through all the trouble of legally changing my name, I wanted to love it, not just like it.

I waited a few months to start the legal process. I had to get a name change packet from the courthouse. This packet was at least an inch thick. I read it from beginning to end before even filling out the paperwork. I read the instructions carefully, using the checklist as a guide for the process. Completing the paperwork was very challenging to me, not because of the legal wording but because of the mental agony of tracing back my past to recover every address I ever lived at from the time of birth. Because of my addiction to men, I moved over and over again. I had a lot of addresses to find! It was emotionally draining to go over my past. I equated it to going to the dentist to have teeth pulled without Novocain, but I kept my eye on the light at the end of the tunnel. This was not about running away or hiding from anyone. I knew that with a name change, there was an opportunity to transcend all my former pain into living with purpose.

Once I finished filling out the paperwork, it needed to be notarized, and then I had to get my electronic fingerprints done. I waited until February 14 to file my petition for a name change with the court for two reasons: one, what better Valentine's Day gift could I give myself than the gift of a new beginning? Secondly, Valentine's Day is my mother's birthday, and what would be a better way to honor her than putting our names, drama, and pain in the past where they belong and creating a new legacy full of possibilities for our family? The moment I filed my petition was one of pure joy and excitement. I still tear up with joy even as I share this with you. After I filed, I took myself to the cutest garden café with beautiful decor and water fountains and celebrated with a blooming flower tea. Boy, have I come a long way with self-love.

Every day after I filed the petition with the court, I checked the mailbox, hoping to receive my court date. When I filed, I was told it could take up to thirty to sixty days. I waited patiently until the sixty-first day, then called the clerk's office to find out the status. The clerk gave me my court date over the phone that day. I did notice that when I filed, I only listed my middle initial, not my entire middle name. I asked the clerk if this could be fixed during the hearing, and he informed me that if I wanted my entire middle name, I would need to file an amendment at least one week before the court date. Ugh... the thought of having to fill out that paperwork again gave me great pause.

After a good night's sleep, I amended the petition and filed it with the clerk. I was going through all this effort and expense to legally change my name; why not do it so I at least have the option of either using my entire new middle name, just the initial, or not at all? After all, I don't intend to change my name again, so I'd better do it right the first time.

My court hearing was held over Zoom. I had no idea what to expect. My dear friends Tracey and Pat came to my house to support me. It was fascinating. Several petitioners, respondents, and attorneys were on the call as a name change falls under family court, which also handles divorces. I waited patiently for the judge to call my name. Then she finally did. She asked me a few questions, and I had to remind myself to answer only what she asked and not go into the story. One of the questions she asked me was if I was changing my name to commit fraud! I had to really hold myself back from responding snidely. I wanted to say, last I checked people who commit crimes don't go through legal channels to legally change their names to commit crimes. In all the crime TV shows I have watched, they buy forged documents. But I realized she was just doing her job and kept my mocking/snarky thoughts to myself. Within two and a half minutes, it was all done! The judge officially ordered my name change. I immediately had the biggest smile, followed by tears of joy. My friends hugged me, and we went to a fabulous French bistro for a celebratory brunch. I felt loved and supported. I am so grateful they witnessed my rebirth.

A few days after the court hearing, I received the signed order from the judge. I then had to go to court to get certified copies because that was key to changing my name on all my legal documents. The first step was going to Social Security. After waiting twenty-four hours, I could take my receipt and go to the DMV. I attempted to do a "walk-in" at several DMVs in the area but was turned away. You needed an appointment for South Florida, and they were booked weeks in advance. Several people also told me that even with an appointment to be prepared to wait for hours. Since I had been waiting for so long already and felt I was living in limbo between my old and new lives, I decided to drive back to my old neighborhood in Lake County, Florida, where I knew I could walk in and be served within minutes.

My gamble paid off! I took a day off and drove to the Tavares DMV (an eight-hour round trip). Upon walking in, I was given a number, which was called before I could walk away from the counter. Within twenty minutes of arriving, I was walking out with my new driver's license. My new license was essential in creating the domino effect for all the other changes. I needed it before I could change my passport, banking, credit cards, TSA (known traveler number for security clearance for airport lines), health insurance, car insurance, and anything else you can imagine. As each new credit card, debit card, and insurance card in my new name came in, it created more space in my life, and it was time to breathe, finally.

I had been lying low in my new hometown because I found it awkward to go out, network, and meet new people, introducing myself as Lorilyn. It became awkward when I had to pay my bill and the credit cards were still in my (old) legal name and often the server would say "Thank you, Claudia," which would leave my new acquaintances confused, so I would have to go through the story. I didn't want to explain or justify myself. Once it was official and all my documents aligned, I was able to create a new experience, standing in the new vibration of my name and fulfilling my life purpose.

Legally changing my name was a lot like giving birth. From conception to completion, it took about nine months. It was, at times, extremely painful and challenging, but in the end, one of the most empowering things I have ever done. It was something I did just for me, and I was the only one who made all the decisions. If something as simple as changing my name can change my life path and allow me to fulfill my life purpose, why wouldn't I at least try?

After all, how many of us get to pick our name intentionally? I love my new name; I love what it means and represents. It doesn't matter whether I can find it on a bicycle license plate!

CHAPTER TWELVE

WHACK-A-MOLE!

Have you ever played Whack-A-Mole? If you don't know what I am talking about, it is an arcade game often found at fairs and game rooms. The player inserts the coins into the machine, and then a furry-looking creature pops up randomly out of different holes. The idea is to hit the mole when it pops up, only for it to reappear coming out of another hole a moment later. The game is an adrenaline-driven fun challenge, but in real life, it is exhausting.

If you remember, earlier I told you that unhealthy relationships showed up in my life in different areas, like work, bosses, friends, and even coaches. When I worked on an area of my life, like potential partners, the same unhealthy relationships would pop up in a different location, just like the game. So even though I was feeling a sense of rebirth after I legally changed my name, I experienced a similar type of game—except it was happening in real life for me.

As I learned about unhealthy relationships and markers of bad behavior, I had become quicker in identifying signs in potential part-ners. Still, when it showed up in work environments and friendships, it often caught me off guard because it didn't look like the animal I knew. I used to jokingly tell my friends that my ego was a drug dealer, but according to Dr. Jospeh Dispenza, I wasn't far off. In his book *Breaking the Habit of Being Yourself*, he explains that when we are used to a particular emotional lifestyle, we will keep re-creating it. Our thoughts and emotions create the chemistry of our body. Our bodies get used to those emotions, and when they don't have the usual chemical response, they re-create scenarios to get it even if it's not healthy. They say in recovery programs the first step to healing is admitting you have a problem. It wasn't until I recognized the pattern of having repeatedly chosen men with my dad's communication style that I could start the recovery work.

Since childhood, I have deeply desired to be part of a family. With so many years in age difference between my siblings and me, I grew up like an only child, and when we did gather as a family and things went wrong, it somehow always ended up as my fault and I was blamed. I felt I was always on the outside looking in. I was so conditioned from my childhood that it was one reason that as life went on and things went wrong in *any* area, I immediately thought it was my fault. I was drawn to men with large families, yet I still felt like an outsider. I craved family so much that in January of 2024, I found a new spiritual church near Pompano Beach. Since I was new to the area and craved being part of a community, I signed up for a class. Over the next eight weeks, I would donate over forty hours of my time and professional talent and close to $2,000 in tithing. I saw the dysfunction within the church management and members, but I stayed anyway because I had committed to volunteering for classes. I told myself I had to complete my commitment to stay in integrity. This was the moment I realized my core values were out of order. Integrity had been my number one core value up until that day. It was then I realized that my personal safety should be my number one core value and that integrity starts with me first.

I decided to remove myself from the toxic situation and express myself, my experience, and my feelings to the new minister. I took my time and wrote a list of everything I needed to bring to completion for my well-being. I made sure the list was based on facts and not emotions. I sat with my list until I reached a place of emotional neutrality where every thought was expressed. When I met with him, he listened with intention and compassion. He didn't try to dismiss my experience or tell me my experience was something different. I felt complete and could mark that chapter of my life done. What I took away from this mole that popped up in my life around my need for community was that I don't need to search for community. I just needed to be me and do the things I love, and my true community will come to me. I got so caught up in being in a "family" that I attracted my childhood dysfunctions all over again. What I also realized is that I have already been blessed with a family. My two wonderful sons and all my beautiful friends are the family I choose. Not only does it feel good to choose who is in my life, it is empowering to break the cycle of addiction and create healthy, loving, supportive relationships.

As the church drama was coming to end, I met with a potential strategic-planning client. My body knew in that meeting that it was not a good fit. There was a pit in my stomach. During that meeting, one of the individuals was extremely difficult; they opposed everything I said and even told me how they had sat in several strategic-planning meetings before and had no idea how it would save their organization, which was on the brink of closing its doors. They wanted to know how to save it without doing the work. I even boldly commented that I didn't know what salmon did to deserve a life of swimming against the current, but I am not a salmon. I told them I didn't believe they were open to the process and that I wasn't a good fit for them. Quickly after, they tried to assure me that what they said wasn't what they said, otherwise known as gaslighting. They insisted they would be open to the process. I left that meeting with a clear inner *no*.

Later that same evening, I got an email from the difficult one assuring me that how they came off wasn't a clear representation and that their organization needed my services, and they hoped I would consider moving forward with them. The next day, the other difficult person texted me, "I hope we didn't scare you off." Because I have been conditioned in unhealthy relationships my entire life and because I still want to believe in people—and I could use the money —I went against my intuition and took the job on, even when over a decade ago, they worked with my mentor in a strategic-planning session and never applied anything they had created. They swore to me that it was because of their old leadership and that things would be different with the new leadership. I have never had such a terrible experience with a client. They challenged my work and sometimes completely ignored my advice. It got so hostile that I had to remind them we were on the same team and that it was supposed to be a collaboration. The people-pleaser in me, trying to create peace and a win-win scenario, worked extra consulting hours and provided services not in the contract. I even made myself available after hours and on weekends to accommodate their schedule until I received a call on a Saturday morning. I only allowed the call because I thought it was about an email about the agenda. When I got on the call, it was nothing like I imagined. Difficult person #2 proceeded to tell me how to do my job and how, at the end of the day, they were paying me, so I needed to do what they wanted. I was furious. I don't like being threatened in any circumstance, and just because you are paying someone doesn't give you the right to treat them poorly.

Meanwhile, everything that he was demanding had already been provided to him; he just didn't read it. Of course, I was now over my limit of tolerance. I felt I had been more than generous, and none of them were qualified to do my job, or they wouldn't have hired me. He didn't like my tone, and I told him if he didn't like my tone, he should have called me during my regular business hours and not on my personal time, knowing that I only had a few minutes. Once again, I offered for us to consider our contract complete where we were. Once he realized he already had the details and hadn't read them, he quickly tried to back out of the conversation. We agreed that we would complete our contract and move forward. After I hung up the phone, I made a commitment to myself. I promised I would only do what was required of me to fulfill my end of the contract and that I would only respond to any future calls or emails during my regular business hours. The days leading up to their Strategic Planning Retreat had me unsure of what to expect. I felt like I was walking on eggshells. We had a few email exchanges that eased some of my anxiety, as it seemed that we both were doing our best to get through this commitment. The retreat was a success. Not only did we accomplish our goal, we did it with time to spare. I received a text from both "Difficulties" thanking me for my hard work, and they acknowledged that they wouldn't have accomplished all they did without me. I felt validated and angry at the same time. Why did it have to be that hard in the first place?

There had been red flags all over, and even with all my hard work over the years, with one word—yes—I was back in an unhealthy relationship. I chose to believe a stranger based on their word—and my perception of needing money—over my inner knowing and intuition. For most of my life, I have tried to convince people I am worthy, and here I was at fifty-two still doing it. My coach tells me I have nothing to prove to anyone at any time, not even to myself! I learned from this experience that I need to trust my intuition and stick to my no's.

It sounds easier than it is. Growing up, my no's didn't have meaning, so in my adulthood, I have been conditioned to let others walk all over my boundaries. This painful experience showed me that not standing in my truth no longer serves me or anyone. I now have a clear marker for my no, and I will do my best moving forward to honor my boundaries. I can't expect anyone to honor my boundaries if I don't first do it myself.

AT THE SAME TIME I WAS DEALING WITH THE CONSEQUENCES OF THE above business decision, another mole popped up in another area of my life. This one took me on an emotional roller-coaster ride, as I didn't see it coming. I was working with a client, an association, and had a successful strategic-planning session with them. I worked closely with the association's board president, Sarah, who also ran a nonprofit organization, and we got along great. She was helpful during the process and had picked up the cost of our meals over our meetings, so I told her that when we completed our contract that I would like to take her out for dinner as friends, to thank her. We scheduled an evening—just weeks after my date with Patrick, if you're keeping track.

As I was getting ready for our dinner appointment, I noticed I had butterflies and a sense of excitement and nerves. I thought that was weird. We met for dinner, and Sarah was very open to sharing food. One of the things I appreciate with all my friends is sharing food so we can try several items from the menu. This night, as usual, we had interesting conversations, laughs, and delicious food. There was a moment when we reached across the table and touched hands. Before we knew it, over three hours had passed and we were the only ones left in the restaurant when the manager came over to politely ask us to leave. It was lightly raining as we left the restaurant. Sarah walked me to my car and asked if she could kiss me. I was caught off guard; it was a gentle kiss on the lips, and then she left.

I was confused. What just happened? I have never kissed a woman, nor have I ever been attracted to one. I have always believed that love is love, and I support other people's choices. I had developed an even better understanding of this concept during my yoga teacher training when, on the first day, our teacher led us through a guided Yoga Nidra meditation into a deep state of relaxation. After the meditation, she asked us, "While you were in meditation, did you happen to notice your age? Did you notice your gender? Did you notice what color your skin is?" As I pondered her questions, I responded no, I didn't notice any of that. She said, "That is because we are all just souls." If it wasn't for this experience that deepened my appreciation that we are all just souls and that love is love regardless of genders, I probably would have not been open to the possibility of a relationship with a woman.

That conversation with my yoga teacher was why, when Sarah asked me to go to dinner again two days later, on a Sunday night, to discuss the possibility of exploring a romantic relationship, I said yes. Part of me was just as curious as I was confused. The same feeling of butterflies and a romantic nervousness in my belly were back as I got ready for our date. I thought, maybe my body knew something I didn't know yet, but I couldn't interpret what it was telling me.

We went to dinner at a restaurant that she remembered me saying was on my wish list. I was impressed because no man had ever paid that much attention. Over dinner she told me that she had planned on hiring me to work with her nonprofit's staff, but now it would be a conflict of interest. I was a bit taken aback and disappointed in myself. I have always been able to keep my professional and personal lives separate. As the evening wore on, we once again shared delicious food, captivating conversations, and belly laughs. During our conversations over dinner, she suggested that we become friends over the next three months and see how it goes before we have any kind of physical intimacy. It was because of that conversation I felt comfortable with us going back to my place for a more private conversation and to avoid being kicked out of another closing restaurant. She went to the Publix liquor store and picked up a bottle of wine to enjoy while we talked.

My home is a sacred and safe place to me, especially after my assault. Before Sarah, I had never entertained any potential partners at my house. At first it felt like having any other girlfriend over for a chat. When she accidentally spilled her red wine all over my dusty-rose couch, she made an uncomfortable comment. When I ignored her comment, she repeated, "I would like the opportunity to stain your couch in a different way." Now I was really uncomfortable. It quickly went from us talking to a make-out session. When I tried to change the focus, she tried to renegotiate her promise earlier in the restaurant about waiting three months. She wanted to know if we could at least cuddle with some caresses. It was all happening so quickly. She made another comment that made me uncomfortable as we talked; she leaned in, sniffed my chest, and told me how intoxicating my smell was. As I was thinking I needed to end this, she said, "I can feel your heat." I was done. I told her that the evening was over and asked her to leave. She seemed unaware of how uncomfortable her actions had made me feel, but she did leave without being asked twice.

The next day, Monday, she texted and asked me if we could just go to the beach and talk while the sun set from five to seven p.m. the following Sunday, which happened to be Easter Sunday. I said yes because the beach is a public area, and it would be only for two hours; I figured it would be okay. Then I would have an opportunity to let her know how I had felt the previous night. Then she texted, "Maybe we can grab dinner after." Then, another text later, asking if she could come earlier? "It might be nice to play by the water for a while."

She knew I was writing this book and that Sundays are my writing day. She went on to say how she wouldn't bother me while I worked. I asked her what time she had in mind, and she replied two o'clock. Wait what? Our plans had gone from meeting for two hours around sunset to a possible dinner, and now they were beginning at two o'clock? Since I felt that she had not respected any of my boundaries this far, I told her that I would meet her at the beach later as we originally planned. But I was angry that I was even being put in this situation, so I told her I had to think about it and that I would let her know closer to the end of the week.

Over the next few days I experienced deep rage! I am talking about the kind of rage that is an out-of-body experience when you aren't even aware of your actions or have any sense of their consequences. When I was driving to a store in an area I wasn't familiar with, my rage was already just below my surface. I was confused and lost. I stopped in a parking lot, looked both ways, and just as I was about to go, a car came out of nowhere. The driver blew his horn and made several obscene hand gestures to me. He did have the right of way, but his response to me set me off. I made several of my own hand gestures back at him. He stopped his car and put it in reverse, and I thought, *Bring it on, motherfucker.* At that point, I was so enraged that I had no idea of the potential harm I might have caused myself. I am sure the female passenger in his car is the only reason we didn't have an in-person altercation.

The very next day, I was again flipping off a white male driving a very expensive car. Because I live between the intercoastal and the ocean, everything about driving is timing. To avoid traffic, you have to time your travel around drawbridges, trains, and construction. I was coming home and hit the drawbridge in its up position. Catching the drawbridge up can turn a seven-minute ride home into at least twenty minutes or more. I was close to the bridge on the main road when it went up. There are side roads where the merging traffic would back up, waiting for the bridge to open and merge into the main road. The guy I flipped off was in the back of that line and decided he didn't want to wait, so he crossed a parking lot and wedged between me and the car in front of me. I found myself rambling on about white privileged men feeling entitled to take or do whatever they wanted. Once again, I was filled with blinding rage! So much so that I refused to let him get in front of me. I figured, I have a Honda, and he has a Porsche. I am on the main road, and he is trying to merge. In the moment, it seemed I had the upper hand and challenged him to dare me as I continued to scream and make hand gestures. The car behind me let him in. As I approached the road where people were patiently waiting to merge, I let a bunch of the cars out in front of me, all while I was thinking, *Take that, jackass!*

When I got home and the rage started to subside, I was asking myself who am I? Where is this coming from? This is not my normal behavior. At first I thought it was from feeling confused about my sexuality and not feeling safe enough to share my recent experience with anyone. I felt like a pressure cooker ready to explode. I knew I had to do something to release my emotions. The next day, I asked my dear friend Tracey to go on a walk and talk with me. Tracey never judges me, and we have been through a lot together in the many years of our friendship. Even with our beautiful friendship, I was still scared to share the intimate societal moral dilemma I was experiencing. I was nervous leading up to the day of our walk. I even talked about everything but what I wanted to share, until I finally told Tracey.

Of course she was supportive and nonjudgmental. She held a

beautiful space where I could hear my thoughts. She helped me recognize that my boundaries were not being respected by Sarah. Then Tracey said something profound. She told me that if Sarah was a guy behaving the way she was, I would have noticed it immediately and would not have let it go on so long. It was because Sarah was a woman, I didn't notice the red flags or unhealthy behavior. Holy cow! She was right. I have gotten so good at recognizing the flags with potential male partners, I would have ended it right away. After all, I just walked away from the very delicious, tall, dark, and handsome Patrick.

My conversation with Tracey had released enough of the emotional pressure that I could start making decisions to support myself. I made an appointment for the Saturday before Easter Sunday with my coach to dive deeper into what I was experiencing. I then reached out to Sarah and canceled our plans. I sent her a text that said, "I am canceling our plans for Sunday, as I need some space to process all the emotions. Thank you for understanding and for giving me the space I need." She replied and said, "Absolutely. I completely understand. Should you want to talk, I'm here. Should you not want to talk, I will respect that as well!" Whew, I could breathe again, or so I thought.

Days later, I received a text from Sarah. "Hello. Are you okay? I know you asked that I respect your wishes, and I have. I've been wondering how you are. Is it possible to build a friendship? How would you like to proceed from a professional perspective? I am sorry if I've caused you any pain." What the actual fuck? Reading that text made my blood boil!

First you do not respect my wishes if you text me when I've asked for time. What that means is "I respected your wishes until mine became more important." It was another clear violation of my boundaries. Then she asked if we could be friends, and she didn't even stick to her own boundaries the first time she offered that during our dinner date.

Last but not least, there's the professional perspective! She had already told me I ruined any future opportunities because it would be a conflict of interest, but now we can discuss that? The entire text was manipulative. Posing as if you have concern for someone by asking them how they are even after they clearly say not to is manipulation. It is to coerce someone into responding out of guilt to let you know they are okay. I was furious that I was being "forced" to answer.

I did have a choice to ignore her, but abusive relationships have so deeply conditioned me that I did answer her. I told her I had planned to reach out after I returned home from a work trip. That I was trying to focus on my clients. Since we still have shared professional connections, I wanted to keep our situation neutral. I told her we could try to be friends and I would not forgive myself if I ruined our professional relationship.

While it was not even clear if we still had a professional relationship, in an abusive relationship the person uses this power as leverage to manipulate their victim. I was trying to defuse the situation by saying we could be friends when I really didn't want to be, in an attempt to keep the peace so our mutual professional relationships would not be impacted. That was exactly what I would have done when I was younger. I would think it was my fault, therefore I would have to suck it up and fix it.

I was already beating myself up from our dinner conversation when she told me she could no longer hire me, assuming it to be my fault. She then told me that "professionally, we are strong." What? This contradiction and confusion is classic Manipulation 101. She then went on to say to me that the association (where she is the board president) I previously worked with was considering hiring me for another project.

She then continued to say that we could only be friends if we were willing to have an honest conversation. Communication is the pillar of my business; I was offended by her comments. I live by what I teach, whether from the stage, in a workshop, with my sons, or with my friends. I responded that the only conversation she would have with me would be honest to the extent I have processed it.

Trying to save face and walk away from the situation with minimum damage to my professional life, I told her I was still seeking professional help to sort through it and would happily support the association however I could.

WHEN SOMEONE WHO HAS CONTROL IN AN UNHEALTHY RELATIONSHIP realizes they are losing control, they resort to different tactics. One of those methods is called "hoovering" and is named after the Hoover vacuum. It is designed to grab you and suck you back into the relationship. It is usually focused on something the victim wants or desires. Previously, men would use the fairy-tale ending to get me to come back; in this situation, Sarah tried to suck me back in with the promise of additional work with our mutual professional relationship. Of course, I noticed the work wasn't for the nonprofit organization she ran but the one she volunteered for.

It gets weirder. The next day, after she told me that we could be friends and that we were professionally strong, Sarah unsubscribed from my monthly newsletter. I think she was wiping the sweat off her brow, just like I was. We both wanted out while saving our reputations.

Then, a week later, she dared to text me and tell me about a book she read that she felt would help my business. Wow, was I ticked off? First, she had never even completed one of my communication programs. Second, she unsubscribed, so why was she sharing information suddenly? Was it from a place of really caring, or was it a way to send me a message that my work lacks something? My ego, which has a black belt in kicking my ass, wanted to latch on to it and tell me how I sucked, my work sucked, and Sarah was pointing to that. A text like that is another method to hoover me back in. I decided not to engage any further.

I'll spare you the details, but this does have a happy ending. In fact, I was hired by the association again for the new project and Sarah had stepped down as the association's president, which meant she would not be part of the special project. That was a win for me, as I normally would have shrunk to make myself invisible to avoid further pain. I feel proud that I took a stand for myself, created new boundaries, and held them. I have never mixed business and pleasure before, and I have promised myself—man or woman—that I will never do it again. Lesson learned!

What I also realized was that the butterflies and nervousness I had been experiencing weren't a sign of a potential amazing relationship; they were my body warning me that it was the same unhealthy fairy tale from my childhood. It was my body's chemical reaction, creating the very drug I had been addicted to most of my life. Those are the same feelings and emotions I have felt every time I entered an unhealthy relationship. I didn't recognize it sooner because I hadn't seen her coming! I had never had an experience with a woman, and it caught me off guard. Since then I have been more discerning with anyone who comes into my life. I watch their behavior. Do they respect my boundaries? Do they do what they say they will do? Do they seem interested in me only physically? Do they dig for all the dirt from my life during the conversation? All those behaviors I used to be flattered by, now I realize they are markers for an unhealthy relationship.

As for my rage, my first coach often told me, "If you can feel it, you can heal it." Our emotions signal us to look deeper behind them to see what is happening. When I sat with my rage, I discovered that I had buried all my anger deep within my body and soul. All the interactions I was experiencing at once with my church, Sarah, work, aggressive drivers, etc., had churned up the gunk. The more uncomfortable I got emotionally, the more anger spewed out sideways like a volcano lying dormant and then exploding uncontrollably everywhere. As my emotions spilled out, I noticed the anger was geared at all the white privileged men in my life who had taken advantage of me. But beneath that was the anger at myself for allowing it to happen. Victims often blame themselves for other people's bad behavior because they are groomed to do so. As a child or even an adult operating out of survival, I knew nothing different from my upbringing. If I continue to be angry and abusive with myself for what I didn't know, then I am no better than anyone who has ever abused me. Now that I have awareness and tools, it is time to heal and make new choices to match/align with my new name.

With the universe providing me with opportunities from every angle of life, I felt I was failing all the tests. My ego was having a feast on all the ways it could tell me what a crappy job I was doing. "Look at you! All these years of self-work, therapy, coaching, and you are still falling for the same shit."

During a much-needed girls' night with my dear friend Lindsay, we were eating and catching up on life. I shared all those stories of my failure. She asked me, "What if the universe is not testing you but giving you opportunities to heal?" Wow, that was an empowering shift in perspective! I decided to try that lens on and discovered she was right. As I started to process, I realized I had gotten to speak my truth with the church and my strategic-planning client. I also got to re-create new boundaries. With the church, I unsubscribed from the mailing list, blocked unhealthy contacts, and removed myself from any further interaction. With the strategic-planning client, I decided to only communicate with them during my business hours and to do what was legally required of me from our contract. With Sarah, my ego wanted to confront her and call her out badly, but I decided to follow my core values and put my safety first. I knew if I tried to converse with her, I would be wasting my energy and opening myself up to an opportunity to get manipulated and gaslighted again.

For all my fellow people-pleasers, I am about to say something that might just blow your mind: I reminded myself that no response is a response. It is okay to put ourselves first and not engage—not in a way that avoids a situation but from a place of empowerment—choosing to put yourself first in front of the needs of others, especially people who aren't healthy for us.

My younger self hadn't had the knowledge of what was happening; I was being groomed for manipulation and control, which was just part of my growing up. Now that I know what it is and how to identify it, I can make better decisions. I also have a new awareness of the need to use discernment not just in potential partners but in all areas of my life. I may still end up in unhealthy relationships, but the amount of time I spend in them is dramatically less, and the recovery is quicker. I would love to say that I now fully get it and will never have one of these "moles" in my life again. But it is safe to say there could be opportunities in my future until I have healed.

In recovery programs, they often say that you can never have another drink, cigarette, or whatever the addiction is again. I often wondered if that applied to relationships as well. I would love for nothing more than to experience a healthy relationship in this lifetime, and what I realize is that relationship must start with me.

CHAPTER THIRTEEN

BURN, BABY, BURN

A groovy tearoom called Soulful Steep was one of my favorite places to go while living in South Florida. They had over fifty teas to select from and delicious locally baked goods and food. Every corner had a unique seating nook to hang out in—beautiful art for sale from local artists hung on the walls. There is even a salt room and boutique where you can find a special, unique gift. I often went there with my laptop to write because I found the atmosphere inspiring. The owners, Christina and John, are down-to-earth and have big hearts. They wanted to create a space for healing and community. They would often hold fun live events with music, Speed Friendship Networking events, and even a seventies disco-themed evening.

Christina introduced me to Whitney at one disco event. Whitney and I hit it off right away, and our conversation flowed easily. We quickly became friends over the next several months. I really enjoyed our new friendship because we had a lot in common, and we were both single. During one of our conversations about relationships, Whitney introduced me to the Burned Haystack Dating Method (BHDM).

The Burned Haystack Dating Method was created by Jennie Young, PhD. Her degree is in Rhetoric, and she teaches women and nonbinary folks how to apply Critical Discourse Analysis to dating profiles to expose unhealthy patterns in online dating profiles. She created this methodology because she was on her journey to finding her partner, and one night she googled how to find a needle in a haystack. The answer was to burn it, which is how the method got its name. Part of her method is what she refers to as Block to Burn (B2B), meaning if you are looking to date someone without children, anyone who comes across your profile that has kids is immediately B2B, or if they had one of the patterns that Jennie teaches to avoid—like profiles that claim they want candidates who are "drama free," which often means they themselves are potentially full of drama. Another reason you might B2B is if you are speaking to someone and they get sexual before you even meet with them; or if the conversation doesn't progress after a week, etc. She shares various rules, but the idea is to block anyone who does not align with what you are looking for or who is inappropriate. The idea is that you are burning the haystack to find the needle, aka a potential healthy partner.

As a researcher and scientist in my own right, I fell into the rabbit hole of all the information she was freely sharing online with 80,000-plus people at the time. Her findings fascinated me, and I found it helpful to put scientific terms to patterns I had recognized throughout my recovery.

I immediately started applying the BHDM in my life even though I was not actively dating on apps. But like any good junkie, I always had a stash of "backup" men in case I had a relapse and needed male attention. I had several men in my life I would communicate with on occasion to feed my addiction when I started to Jones for some attention. There was Philip (another Italian), whom I'd met back in my twenties at the nightclub where I worked before meeting Vinnie. He lives in New York City, and from time to time, if I happened to be in town, we would meet for a steamy evening of sex. Over the years, we have reached out to each other and caught up. Like several other men, he fed me breadcrumbs, always promising to visit me. Still, here we are, thirty years later, and he never followed through even though I found out that on several occasions he had been in Florida, not too far from me, and never told me.

Then there was Larry, my friend with benefits I made in December 2021. We enjoyed our mutual emotionally stimulating conversations, but we did not have a whole lot in common, especially when it came to personal core values. Since neither of us wanted a relationship, we agreed that when we were in the same location and both felt like having intimacy, we would meet up. At the time, it was what I needed. After having several relationships back-to-back with men who could not perform for one reason or another, my self-esteem and sexual confidence were almost nonexistent. Our agreement was built on my needs and desires for me to explore my sexuality with someone I trusted. It worked because, with so many differences, we had no chance of being a couple. It allowed me to have an experience without the risk of it becoming an emotional connection.

And I must mention George! Talk about a "Stella got her groove back" moment. I met George on a cruise ship in January of 2024. He was younger than me and had a feminine quality to him, so when he struck up a conversation with me on the first night of the cruise in the club, I was caught off guard when he asked me if I had ever dated someone younger. I have dated men a year or a couple of years younger than I am but never one that would qualify me as a cougar. I laughed at his question and thought he was kidding. He then told me it was his preference to date a more mature woman. George and I danced the night away and ended up having some great conversations, to my surprise. We did end up kissing that night. Over the next several days we would find time to connect for authentic conversations. On the evening before disembarking, George and I had some quality sexy time together! It was hot, steamy, and a night I will not forget. I felt empowered by our interactions and realized I had gained my sexual self-confidence back. George shocked me on the last morning of the cruise by finding me and saying goodbye. We stayed in touch regularly after the cruise for several months. George was planning to come and visit me in Florida sometime over the summer.

Then there was the local driver for a community electric golf cart rideshare named Michael. He was also an Italian from NY. He had the hots for me, but once I found out he was only separated and not divorced, I was no longer open to that possibility. But I liked having an inside connection to get a ride downtown, especially during peak times. Shamefully, I kept a connection with him for convenience and as a backup plan in case I had a relapse and needed a fix of male attention, if I was honest with myself.

It was a Saturday evening in June when I took a cocktail down to the beach to contemplate the BHDM while grounding my feet in the warm sand, listening to the ocean as I watched the sunset change the color of the sky. At that moment I had clarity. My backup boys were straws of hay in my stack. I knew that I was holding on to them for the wrong reasons and that if I ever wanted to experience a healthy relationship, I needed to release them or, as Jennie Young would say, "B2B." I mindfully, honestly, and lovingly sent a personalized text to each one of them, letting them know that our relationship had reached completion for me, thanking them for the lessons I learned from them, and that I was wishing them well on their journey of life.

Phil from NY didn't even use any energy to respond. He just sent a heart emoji. I was not surprised because I had done most of the labor in our friendship over the years. I blocked Philip before I deleted him from my contact list. Michael respected my boundary of having no further contact for about forty-eight hours before texting me, asking me if I was home and could he swing by. Um, no. Goodbye. He was a definite B2B—inside rideshare connection or not. Larry waited to respond until the next day, saying he learned to wait for emotional clarity before responding to me. He wanted to be mindful and present with his response. George seemed confused by my decision as my text did come out of nowhere. He said he was planning a visit but was *so* understanding and loving in his response. I had finally burned my secret stash.

During my coffee shop girl time with Whitney, we would share stories of our experiences and any insights gained from the Facebook group for the Burned Haystack Dating Method. Whitney was actively dating on dating apps where I met people more organically while doing things that I enjoyed, such as dancing, art exhibits, etc. One day during our conversation, Whitney suggested that I try online dating to test the Burned Haystack Dating Method. She knew how to pique my interest when she said I could do it "for science."

Over the next few days, I contemplated signing up for Facebook dating. After all, it was free and "research," right? Jennie Young suggests to the people who follow her to write their profiles from a brutally honest but positive place and not to tell potential dates what they are looking for, because that is like giving them a map to manipulate the outcome. Being a writer, I carefully crafted mine and then sent it to Whitney for feedback. Here is the final version we created:

I have a quirky sense of humor and at times can be socially awkward. I appreciate meaningful conversations and a whimsical spirit. I am currently making an attempt to learn Spanish since my nest is now empty, and I have the freedom to explore my interests and passions, like going to Argentina to learn tango. I love to dance although sometimes I dance to my own beat.

I love my career; it takes me to new, exciting destinations that I might not have explored on my own. I am a certified yoga teacher, but I don't teach, although I do use some tools in my work. Yoga provides me with an opportunity to learn, grow, and slow my busy brain down.

I guess you might not find it shocking to learn that I am spiritual and open-minded. I believe women have the right to choose, love is love, and Black lives matter.

Even though I am an independent woman, I have some old-fashioned tendencies and appreciate it when doors are held open and seats are pulled out.

Ever see a dog with its head out the window enjoying life to the fullest? That is how I feel when I ride a motorcycle. I have my license, but I can also be a great passenger.

I hardly have time to watch TV as I love to explore new areas, do anything related to the arts, learn new things, and oh my goodness, I can't pass up a great bookstore.

I appreciate great atmospheres, the occasional tasty cocktail, and delicious food, a plus if there is live music. I geek out over writing Google reviews for extraordinary experiences. What was your last review-worthy dining experience?

I was proud of my bio. Whitney and I then carefully selected recent photos that showed me doing various activities and events I love. I chose a picture Whitney had taken of me at one of our meetups at the tearoom. I loved it because it was all natural. I didn't have my hair or makeup done. It was me unapologetically standing in my power. I figured if it were my main profile picture, it would show my authentic self, not some dolled-up version of me, and if someone saw the natural me, were interested, and checked all the BHDM boxes, we would be good to go!

Because I have learned to follow my Human Design strategy, I slept on it overnight. The next day, I decided to go for it and post my profile. In the past, I would sign up for a dating service and pay the fees, only to be annoyed within a week by the amount of time and energy it took to meet less-than-par potential partners. I would often delete the account soon after I opened it. Because Jennie Young knows the dating apps are gamified and that they want to keep us on them longer, she advises her followers to only check their profile for messages twice a day for ten to fifteen minutes and not to allow the process to consume all their time and precious energy. This time I felt prepared with an honest profile, great photos, and a new perspective on handling my profile.

I had to download the Facebook app to my phone because it is the only way to use Facebook for dating. For years, I refused to have an account, let alone have the app on my phone. Still, I wanted to test the method for my own experience, so I did, knowing that I would use the discipline I have built up over the past few years of not having the app at all and would not need to check my profile every second to see how many people liked my recent post. I was ready to go until I realized my beautiful, crafted profile was too long for the Facebook dating app. They only allowed five hundred characters! I had to go in and edit. It was a challenge, but I wanted the most important things to stand out in my profile. It ended up looking like this:

Empty nester with a quirky sense of humor and can be socially awkward at times. I believe women have the right to choose, love is love, and Black lives matter. Even though I am an independent woman, I have some old-fashioned tendencies, like appreciating when doors are held open. Ever see a dog with its head out the window enjoying life to the fullest? That is how I feel when I ride a motorcycle. I have my license, but I can also be a great passenger.

I wanted to express that I didn't have young children and did not want someone who did. I wanted them to know that I am a feminist liberal with boundaries. I was not looking for sexual hookups, and I wanted them to know I was work if they wanted to get intimate with me. I wanted them to know I am independent but willing to work as a team.

I did not waste my time swiping on profiles. Jennie Young encourages her followers to no longer do the emotional work for men and that if a man couldn't take the incentive to ask for the first meeting and at least offer a plan, they were an immediate B2B because that foreshadowed the relationship's future. I had already experienced enough of that, so I was committed to her process. She also encourages us to match the energy of the interaction. If the person interested in you says hi and they match your values and desires, you would only say hi back. I looked to see who had messaged me. If they didn't get B2B and caught my interest, I would interact with them only at their level of effort. I did a lot of burning of my haystack and minimized my interactions. Following the BHDM helped me conserve my time and energy.

I had one guy who made it past all the filters I was using to have an in-person meeting. I had my rule of not giving my phone number out before an in-person meeting. This man was doing all the right things. He agreed to my rule about my phone number, requested the first date, and offered to come to meet me for coffee in a location of my choice. On our date day, he even communicated via the dating app that he was stuck in traffic and would be a few minutes late. Wow, this guy was looking good, right? But because I have learned a lot, I knew not to let my guard down, to keep my eyes and ears open, and observe how my body responded.

We went inside and ordered our coffee at the counter. He offered to pay. I was disappointed when he completely ignored the tip option, then quickly walked away from the register mid-transaction to use the restroom, which left the young woman cashier to turn the iPad back around to her and hit No Tip to complete the transaction. An immediate flag for me, but he did warn me he had to use the restroom when he got there, so I only gave it a yellow flag because he did drive a distance, and I have had those experiences of needing to use the restroom *now*. I tipped the cashier and said, "Well, we will see how this goes, but right now I don't think there will be a second date."

During our conversation, he was aloof about what line of work he was in and even intentionally tried to misdirect me. He then went on to tell a story about a woman who was married and got pregnant by someone else that I was not surprised to learn was a story about himself. I won't go into the sordid details, but over the course of our meeting, he shared his "victim story" with his narcissist ex-wife. If someone throws out the term narcissist on a first date, it's my cue to drop everything and run. Then he was elusive and deflected my questions around his line of work; he ultimately admitted to being a (boring) hedge fund bean counter. He quickly shifted directions again. This time he tried to pull out the big guns and impress me with all his money by showing me photos of his homes.

I was getting ready to end the date when he made a statement alluding to the fact that everyone has the same opportunity as he did to achieve his level of success. I shockingly asked him, "Are you kidding?" just like my mom, in shock, had responded to the bank robber! I then followed up with, "You *do* know I am a feminist liberal, right?" Now he looked like *he* was in shock. He quickly pulled out his phone and pulled up my dating profile. He read it aloud and completely skipped my line, "I believe women have the right to choose, love is love, and Black lives matter." I said, "Wow, you just missed it. Back up."

Once he read the line, he demanded that I convince him why I disagreed with his statement. I tried to be open to the possibility that maybe, just maybe, this guy would be willing to hear what I have to say, but he would interrupt me as I was speaking to mansplain things to me. I realized this man was not going to listen to a word I was saying. I interrupted him, told him the date was over, and tried to thank him for his time, but he then made a ridiculous statement (which I refuse to share in my book). Having had enough of his behavior, I told him it was not my job to convince or educate him and left. Before I even got to the corner, I was on the dating app blocking his profile. Thank goodness I hadn't broken my rule and given him my number.

A version of myself not so long ago might have allowed me to look past his behavior because of his wealth and my belief that I needed a man, but not this time. The next day, I had a coaching session with my coach, Charllotte. I told her I was annoyed at myself for staying as long as I did on the date. Charllotte then asked me a series of questions: "How long did you stay with Jack?" I responded, "For almost two years." She quickly pointed out my improvement from a couple of years to a cup of coffee. It was at that moment that I realized that I had finally broken my addiction and loved myself more than any man or perceived circumstances.

After that coaching session, I deleted the app. My research was complete. Like Dorothy from *The Wizard of Oz*, I'd found my needle in the haystack: "It was in me the whole time." I had finally found my healthy and loving relationship with myself. I was ready for a new dance with life!

CHAPTER FOURTEEN

A NEW DANCE

In my earlier years, touch was one of my primary love languages and not necessarily in a sexual way. I craved to be held and to feel loved. It fed my addiction that I believed I needed a man. Now I look for ways to get safe touch. Safe touch includes things like massages, pedicures, and dancing.

Dancing has always brought me joy since I can remember, but after my rape, it also became a form of therapy. After my assault in 2018 and before Jack came along, I had a hard time with the thought of intimacy and trust. As part of my healing process, I decided to push myself out of my comfort zone and reclaim dancing as, at one time, it had brought so much joy to my soul. I signed up for salsa classes because it felt like a safe way to dip my toe back into not only dancing but learning to trust again.

My first teacher was kind, and before he knew my "why" for wanting to learn salsa, he would tease me about my need for control and how I was trying to lead. As we danced together, I started to trust him, and one day, I told him that I had experienced an assault and that I wanted to take back my sensuality and learn how to trust, especially men. He said, "Well, you certainly are an overachiever, because salsa is one of the most intimate and sensual dances there is." We both shared a giggle, but he was right! I was pushing my own boundaries.

I had a strong underlying will that would not allow me to give over complete trust, so I struggled with the steps, often stepping on toes or getting my toes stepped on. We started to make progress when my teacher asked me to consider closing my eyes when we danced. Because I could not see where we were going, I had to surrender control and trust that he would keep me safe. We started to make great progress, and I even began to reconnect with the joy I used to feel when dancing.

That progress all came to a screeching halt when my dad passed away and I relocated to North Carolina to care for my mom. When caring for my mom, I barely had time for self-care, much less dancing. Then, when I was settling into my new life with Jack, I was looking for a place to pick up my dancing, but COVID hit, and that was the end of that.

While I dabbled with attending the occasional dance class or social after ending my relationship with Jack and moving back to Central Florida, it did not become predominant until after my last experiment with dating apps and testing the BHDM. Now that the dating experiment was out of the way and I realized how committed I am to my relationship with myself, it was easy to delete the apps and choose me.

I decided to focus on doing other things that brought me joy. I signed up for art classes and attended events like full moon sound baths on the beach. I continued to buy myself flowers and take myself out to dinner. I was finally following my joy and providing myself with what I craved instead of waiting for a man to do it. I had been looking for places to dance since I moved to South Florida, but for some reason, I was unsuccessful, which was hard to believe given the area I lived in. But in May 2024, I saw a Facebook event for dancing in a town square one town over on Mother's Day weekend. I was elated. I didn't know anyone when I went to the event, and I felt out of place and awkward at first. I observed from the sideline for a while before joining a group line dance. While dancing, I met other women with a passion for dancing. They told me about a community center in that town that had aerobic dance classes and invited me to check it out.

That Monday, I went to the class and had so much fun I invested in a membership. Not only did the community center have dance aerobics classes, but they had other classes like yoga, Spanish, etc. Then I discovered their Thursday ballroom social group! When I went to my first session, I was immediately welcomed. Unlike most ballroom classes, there was no assigned teacher; instead, there was a group of people who all loved to dance. Everyone helped each other in various types of ballroom dancing. Between the group's kindness and support, I quickly reconnected with my youthful joy and remembered how much I love to dance.

We did different types of ballroom styles, including rumba, foxtrot, salsa, and my favorite, American tango. I quickly made new friends and enjoyed learning. I enjoyed learning with all my friends from the group, male and female, but there was one gentleman I particularly enjoyed practicing with Jeff. He was tall and slender and had previously taken professional lessons. Jeff was timid and somewhat socially awkward. He asked me out after several weeks of seeing each other at the dance socials.

I was not looking to date, but I decided to go out with Jeff because he was not my usual type, and we shared a passion for ballroom dancing. We met for tea at my favorite tearoom, and after a couple of hours of conversation, he asked me if I would like to grab dinner and continue our discussion. We went to the restaurant next door, and he did everything right. He pulled out my chair; we both are foodies and decided to share a few things from the menu. The conversations were easy, and he walked me to my car at the end of the evening. Wow, for me, that was a completely new and different experience. I had put work into myself and clarified who I was and what I wanted. It appeared that my clarity was leading me in a healthy new direction.

For years, I have facilitated strategic-planning sessions for organizations, helping them to get clear on their mission, values, vision, and creating a plan to bring it into reality. After my last few clients (Chapter 12) and my realization that I no longer wanted to work with just any client but with clients who align with my mission, vision, and values, was when I had not only a professional breakthrough of clarity but a personal one: I saw how to use my methodology that combined strategic planning with the CHAT approach for reaching my personal goals.

I was so excited to experiment with my new insight that I brought the concept to the Women Who Chat community. This community is a mastermind group of women who have participated in and completed the CHAT masterclass and my Compassionate Courageous Conversation program. We each created our life vision—just like a business strategic plan that focuses on each aspect of a business, finances, marketing, etc. We concentrated on the different aspects of our life—health, occupation, relationships (friendships, partners, family, etc.), and free time. We each mindfully crafted our vision in the present tense and shared it in our mastermind groups for feedback and to bring it into reality by speaking it out loud. Having a vision by itself is not enough. Just like an organization, we must have our mission statement, which is our "why." Without our "why," we can lose sight of our vision; it keeps us motivated to move toward our goals and clarity regarding our personal core values if we want our vision to come to fruition.

Our mission and values guide us toward creating our vision. Have you ever played bumper bowling? In bumper bowling, a gate is put up on each side of the alley, preventing the ball from going into the gutter, keeping it on the alley and heading toward the pins. The goal of bowling is getting a strike. The pins are our life vision. To make that vision a reality, we must stay on the alley/path to obtain a strike. So if the left side bumper gate is our mission and the right side is our values, they will keep us on target for our vision. The most important part of having a personal strategic plan is clarifying why we want our vision to come to fruition. Without the why, it is like trying to bowl with a blindfold on and being turned around several times, like pinning the tail on the donkey, knowing that there is a bull's-eye somewhere and blindly fumbling and feeling our way around in hopes that we pin the tail on the correct spot, or in bowling we hit a few pins by luck.

But having our mission defined is only another piece of the puzzle. We must also have clarity on our personal core values. Our personal core values are used to check and balance all our decisions. When you are clear on your core values, when any opportunity arises, whether personally or professionally, and you need to make a decision, you can go back to your plan and see if it aligns with your vision. Does it align with your mission? And does it align with your values? If not, it is a no. Our mission, values, and vision guide our decisions and keep us on the right path to making the life we dream our reality.

Which brings us back to my experience with Jeff. Our date went so well that Jeff asked me for our second date the next day. Jeff was a widower. His wife had passed away two years earlier. Not only did he care for his sick wife, but at the same time, he had cared for his mother as she declined. He lost both his mother and his wife within years of each other. His wife was his only long-term relationship, and he was now discovering who he was outside his role of caretaker and husband.

On our second date, we met for lunch at an Indian buffet. Once again, Jeff did everything right. We sat next to each other on the bench. When we approached the buffet, he handed me my plate. He offered to get my beverages, and when my water glass was almost empty, he would signal a server to ask them to refill it. You might think this is no big deal, but this was all new for me because I usually had to do all those things in my prior relationships. This was the first time someone treated me like I had treated others.

Once again, our conversation flowed easily. Since the restaurant was about to close to switch from buffet lunch to dinner, Jeff asked me if I would like to go to the beach together afterward. Now, all dating experts say not to do this, but I was enjoying myself and decided why not? I only get to live once.

We lived only a few minutes apart, so we both went home and got ready for the beach. We then met and walked from my apartment to the beach. Since we are both a little socially awkward, we decided to go to a restaurant on the beach for the view and a cocktail to take the edge off. While sipping our beverages, he gave me a quick and unexpected peck on my lips. It was so awkward that it was endearing. We then headed to the beach, where he continued to blow my mind with his thoughtfulness. He laid out the blanket and helped me up when we decided to go for a swim. I had lived by the beach and visited it almost every day for eight months, but I never went into the ocean farther than my calves, out of fear, but Jeff guided me out past the rocky bottom. We enjoyed jumping the waves while we talked. At one point, he pulled me into his arms, and we just held each other in silence while observing the beauty of nature.

When we finished our dip in the ocean, he helped me back to our blanket, wrapped me in my towel, and we talked a little more. He had to leave soon as he volunteered at night to watch the sea turtle nests and guide the hatchlings to the ocean. I know, right? Where did I find this guy?

On our walk back to my apartment, there was a truck with a political banner and an adorable little dog propped up in the corner for photos. I love fur babies but did not want to engage in the situation, so I kept my head forward and walked as if I didn't see it. Once we got farther down the block, Jeff said, "I guess you are not a fan?" I asked him to clarify his question because I did not know what he was talking about. He said, "I noticed that you didn't engage that adorable dog, so I am guessing you are not a fan." I was shocked at how in tune this man was with me, from noticing when my water needed to be refilled to helping me brush off the sand. His ability to observe my unspoken behavior was mind-blowing because I have never been on the receiving end of it!

Our relationship included delicious food, dancing, volunteering, and walks on the beach, and I had to pinch myself. It felt like my wish list for a dream partner was becoming a reality. His inventiveness, recent losses, and social awkwardness were why I gave him some passes for questionable behavior that should have been seen as red flags. I would gaslight myself and make excuses for him, like he had not been on a date in over twenty years; he'd had only one partner, and this was his first dating experience since losing his wife.

After a lovely day of cooking, eating, and having an incredibly personal conversation about his relationship with his grown daughter, I felt like we might finally be getting past our quirks. We then went for a walk along the beach, and as we talked, he made a comment that left me so stunned that I could not process my thoughts and articulate any words. He told me he was unsure if he was attracted to my body type and might be more attracted to someone who looks like Barbie. What the actual fuck? We walked back to his place and barely spoke a word. We watched a movie; I'd agreed to stay because I was still shocked. I could not grasp what he'd said and was not paying attention to the movie. I had gone numb. Then he sent me mixed signals as he tried to cuddle and kiss me. I excused myself to his bathroom to cry. As soon as the movie ended, I asked him to take me home.

The short ride home was filled with uncomfortable silence. He entered my house and placed my bag on the table when he walked me to my door. Then he turned to me and said, "I don't know why I say the things I say," and he started sobbing as he sat on my bed. At first my instinct as a recovering people-pleaser was to have empathy and console him as I sat next to him. But then *what?* My inner knowledge kicked in and I asked myself, Why are you comforting him? I stood up and told him I needed him to go, *right now*! I would not pour my energy into someone who violated my personal core values or who didn't have clarity of their own values and life vision. I then quickly escorted him to the door and locked it before he cleared it. I am pretty sure his shirt was caught in the door.

At first I was devastated. It stirred up some of my old shit of not being good enough, smart enough, pretty enough. His comment about wanting a Barbie body reactivated my anorexia nervosa. I felt myself spinning out of control and immediately jumped into self-care mode. I contacted Tracey that night and scheduled an appointment for the next day. Tracey is not only my friend but also a great massage therapist, and she has many modalities to support her clients. Her intuition, ability to hold space, and knowledge of aromatherapy and flower essences helped me from going down a dark path. She noticed that I wanted to be (ironically) like a turtle and pull everything in to avoid feeling the pain, which was precisely how I felt. I was once again shutting myself down because of a man.

After my session with Tracey, I journaled about my experience and realized that, just like with my dad, I was not responsible for Jeff's behavior and that his poor behavior had nothing to do with me. I refused to let that experience take me backward for another minute. After my appointment with Tracey, I took myself for a nourishing meal and headed to my favorite tearoom. I had a soothing herbal tea and a session in the salt room. Himalayan salt rooms are very therapeutic and calming to the nervous system. I placed the eye pad over my eyes, focused on my breathing, and allowed the music to take me into a deep meditation. After my session, I took a cup of tea to go and headed to the beach to finish processing my thoughts and feelings.

I was so proud of myself for the gentle and loving way I handled that experience. Because I had identified my vision, mission, and personal core values, I could easily walk away from Jeff. Once I returned to my emotional neutral, I asked Jeff if he would meet me for a closure conversation, and to my surprise, he agreed. I got to express everything I was processing, and even though I did not get all the answers I sought, I felt complete and ready to move forward.

After my experience with Jeff, I wanted to dive deeper into focusing on myself and what I loved. One of my fellow dancers, Sky, a trained dancer, a fantastic actress, and a spectacular artist, felt I had a natural talent for dancing. With her encouragement, I decided to invest in private lessons. Since I no longer had my dance partner, I found a ballroom studio that held weekly social dance events. I could pay a fee for a host, and I was guaranteed at least every third dance. At first I felt weird because most of the women already knew each other. Then a kind woman named Jeanie invited me to sit at her table. Jeanie told me about several different places where I could dance, and before I knew it, I danced six days a week and sometimes twice a day.

I was enjoying my life and dancing. On a Saturday evening in early September of 2024, I was attending a social dance event at my local ballroom. I was sitting down when I turned my head toward the door and saw an unusual sight: a solo man entering the event. It is common in the United States for women to outnumber men at dancing events, which is why I paid for a host to practice what I was learning in my lessons in a social setting because the chances of dancing with someone randomly are not common. The newcomer was tall, dark, and handsome. I remember the receptionist pointing toward me and the dance floor. He then came over and introduced himself. Not only was he tall, dark, and attractive, but he also spoke with an accent and danced! Holy shit, the old version of me would have gone nuts because he appeared to be my "dream partner wish list" come to life, but since I'd recently had my experience with Jeff, my discernment was in full gear.

Rick was from Canada. He owned a business in town and frequently visited the area. He told me he had not danced in years but wanted to return to dancing.

Knowing how it felt to be the new person at those events, I extended to him the same kindness Jeanie had with me. I told him about all the other opportunities to dance, including the group lessons I was attending the next day. Rick ended up coming to that group dancing lesson, and afterward he asked me if I wanted to check out another ballroom with him. The ballroom he mentioned was a place I had wanted to go and heard so much about. I had not explored that opportunity because I was warned that only the more experienced dancers went there and weren't so kind to beginners like me. I decided to meet him there because at least we both were on the beginner side and could stick together to check it out.

We had a great time at the advanced ballroom club. Since we both were beginners and wanted to learn, we agreed to share the cost of dance classes and practice together. During a Friday-night social, we were taking a group lesson before the open dance when Rick stepped so hard on my toes that my stomach dropped and all color left my face. I immediately felt sick to my stomach with pain. The teacher commented, "You know that hurt," but I sucked it up and finished the class before excusing myself to the restroom for a good cry. The pain was excruciating. Rick was not wearing dancing shoes but regular steel-tip shoes, which was why they hurt so much. I thought he had severed my toes from my foot. He felt awful and apologized. I told him that if he was serious about dance and wanted to continue dancing with me, he needed to invest in dance shoes.

The next day, we went out looking for dance shoes together. My dance friends told me about a few places nearby. He found shoes he liked and purchased them. While we were there, I was looking at women's shoes. They had beautiful high-end shoes. Rick encouraged me to try a pair and then offered to buy them. I tried to decline his offer, even saying that they didn't have my preferred color in stock, but he insisted, saying that it was the right thing to do because he had ruined my shoes by stepping on me constantly. He wasn't wrong, and I was uncomfortable arguing in front of the store clerk, so I gave in. Then I found out he bought me two pairs of shoes! The color that was available now and the color I wanted that was not in stock. Those shoes cost over $200 each. I told him I was uncomfortable with that, but he would not take no for an answer. I should have seen that for the red flag that it was. He clearly did not hear or respect my wishes; he put his desires over mine, which should have been when I ended it.

When we'd been getting to know each other, I had asked him if he was single. He didn't wear a wedding band, and I was curious about his status. Rick responded with the old answer of "It's complicated." He then explained that he and his wife had been separated for years and were living in different rooms, blah, blah. I told him very directly that I do not do complicated or get involved with men who are not legally single. I told him that if he wanted to dance and keep it at friends, I would do that. Rick said he had no problem with that and could honor my boundaries.

You may already see where this is going. During our dancing, he would constantly comment about my beautiful smile and how the movement of my hips was distracting, so he didn't keep his frame and repeatedly stepped all over my toes, which was a metaphor for exactly what he was doing to my boundaries. I'd had enough, between him sending me a text message with a flower emoji and telling me how he missed my smile, then trying to make our dance practice into a movie night in the park, claiming we could practice dancing any night, but when could we see this movie again. What? We were not dating; we were dance partners, period. I told him that we should not be friends anymore or dance. Rick tried to convince me that this was how he talks, even to his male friends, but once again, he did not acknowledge how it landed for me.

After several days, we did end up having a conversation, and we agreed to keep dancing only. Well, that didn't last very long because he did not practice, and after spending all that time and money, it was like showing up each time as if it was the first. His constant stepping on my feet and lack of frame got to me. I told him we should seek other partners because dancing was no longer fun for me.

That Saturday night at the dance social, we arrived separately. He got there after I did and ended up sitting at the same table but with his back to me all night. It was very uncomfortable. At the end of the evening, after most of the people had left, he asked me to dance, and I agreed. As we danced, he told me how dancing with me had taken the fun out of it for him! He said, "Your need to dance perfectly has robbed my joy." Wait what? This is a clear sign of a narcissist taking something you say and then turning it around. In the moment of my emotional charge, I let him have it. I said, "I don't need to dance perfectly, but I do need a partner who isn't constantly stepping on me." I told him dancing with him was like dancing in the movie *50 First Dates* and how annoying it was that he could not retain anything and we had to start each lesson anew. Rick responded, "Wow, look at us ripping into each other." I told him that I had gracefully tried to bring our friendship to closure and that he had chosen a different path, so he got what he got. I immediately changed my shoes and left. I blocked him without further discussion before I even left the

146

parking lot. In case you are wondering, I donated both pairs of shoes and never looked back. I had let him violate my boundaries for the last time. Guess what his communication style was? Yup, he had the same communication style as my dad!

Maybe the earlier version of me would have settled for his bull-shit story and been impressed with his financial status, but that was before I got clear on who I am, what I want, and more importantly, knowing my worth. Now, that is true freedom. I finally felt liberated from my past behaviors and ready to create the life I have always dreamed of.

CHAPTER FIFTEEN

ALL IN

It was the end of June 2024, and I had seemed to make peace with my addiction to men. I was falling deeper in love with myself. It was the first time that I could remember feeling contentment. My life finally felt terrific. I was living in paradise, dancing up a storm, and exploring my interests. I even considered adopting a dog. I saw a term on a Facebook group that someone had posted, "Self-Partnered." It was defined as "someone who is content and fulfilled with themselves and doesn't feel the need to have a romantic partner to feel that way. It can also refer to the practice of treating yourself with the same care and nurturing that you would a romantic partner." That was exactly what I was experiencing at that time of my life. My addiction to male attention was no longer robbing me of my peace.

I was so comfortable, and that was when it hit me! I was about to surrender my life's vision and soul desires. Owning a pet is a long commitment, and I knew that if I adopted a dog, my dreams of global travel would probably never happen.

Since I had created my strategic life plan, which included my life vision, I was committed to saying my vision every day along with personalized affirmations:

I am living my best life following my heart's desires and aligning with my Human Design. I wait for the right people, places, and opportunities to present themselves through my amazing network. I enter these relationships and opportunities correctly, guided by my inner wisdom and waiting for my emotional clarity.

I am grateful for my body, exactly as it is right now. I love every nook and cranny, and I am thankful for every healthy, vibrant cell that gives me breath. I show love and gratitude for my body by listening to its needs and providing delicious, healthy nutrition and rest when needed. Daily rituals like dry brushing, journaling, yoga, meditation, walks on the beach, and playing are love notes to self.

I am blessed with amazing family, friends, and clients who recognize my worth, respect my boundaries, and honor me as my authentic self, as I do for them.

I enjoy spending quality time with my sons as we enjoy conversations that bring us closer together. We do fun things, like pottery, comedy clubs, traveling, and sharing delicious meals.

I have amazing friends who can engage in deep, authentic conversations one moment and be completely silly the next. We enjoy time together, knowing that it is quality over quantity when we connect. We enjoy doing various activities, traveling, and, of course, fine dining.

I have a fantastic life partner. Our core values align, and we hold each other to learning, growing, and being a better version of ourselves each day. We have several interests in common and love listening and dancing to live music across the globe. We enjoy the arts, fine dining, and a healthy lifestyle. We are passionate, affectionate, and have a deep, intimate connection with a healthy sex life. We enjoy traveling, going on retreats, and learning together.

I am fulfilling my soul's purpose by helping people reconcile and blend differences through an understanding of hearts and minds. I follow my intuition to understand and support the people I have the honor of working with. I use my God-given talents of my clever, intelligent use of language and humor to create harmony and coop-eration through harmonious discussion and stimulating conversa-tions. I travel across the globe, delivering keynote presentations and workshops. I am generously compensated and respected for my work. I am constantly being referred, and I am in high demand. I am a best-selling author and hold empowering retreats for women, supporting their authentic selves and sharing with them how to be financially free so they can make decisions that align with their truth.

During my alone time, I enjoy receiving delicious spa treatments, reading, walks in nature, riding my bike, exploring expression through art, and taking myself to new places to enjoy food and people-watching. I invest in myself by continuing my yoga education and other subjects that light up my soul!

Amen!

As I daily recited my vision, I realized that I have often told people that my beach apartment is my favorite place I have lived so far! But I had known the whole time that South Florida was not my final destination. That was when I had to ask myself some tough questions: Was I going to give up my life vision and my soul's call for travel to settle into the "comfortable," or was I going to practice what I teach and put my vision into action?

My lease was up for renewal at the end of October, and having to give a sixty-day notice to my landlord meant I needed to decide what I was doing by the end of August. I had a coaching session with Char-llotte at the very end of June, during which I shared my dilemma with her. We talked about my options and my soul's desire for global travel. After that session, I had a lot to think about, and I wanted to wait until I reached my emotional clarity before making any life-changing decisions.

That conversation with Charllotte opened my mind to possibili-ties. I was tired of my car insurance increasing with no rhyme or reason every time the wind blew. Costs of everything were going up, including health insurance, groceries, and gas. I also didn't like what was happening politically in Florida. I started to wonder what it would look like to take all the money I paid in monthly expenses and travel the world.

The more I thought about it, the more excited I got. I had gone all in on the men in my life and given up everything multiple times, hoping they would provide me the security I believed I needed. I decided why not bet on myself and go all in on me this time? My soul was alive and filled with childlike curiosity. Once I reached my emotional clarity, I started researching how to be a digital nomad. I interviewed several people who lived the lifestyle I was about to embark on. I learned much, including many things I needed to do to prepare, like applying for Global Entry, learning what cell phone plans work best, and how to avoid international fees for banking while traveling.

At first I thought I would do a checked bag, a carry-on, and a personal item. When interviewing a gentleman who had traveled to all 193 countries, he told me not to let my luggage outnumber my hands, especially as a woman traveling alone. He only traveled with a backpack. I decided I would travel with a carry-on suitcase and a backpack. It took me several weeks to purchase my luggage because my philosophy was to find the strictest airline luggage requirements for Europe and buy a suitcase and carry-on item that met those regu- lations. My thought was that I did not want to invest in luggage twice. Plus that also meant I would not waste money checking my bag if it was too big for the airline's requirements. When my new suitcase and backpack arrived, it was a rude reality check! They were much smaller than I realized.

As I looked at my new luggage and looked around my apartment, I realized I had a lot of releasing to do. I started a countdown in my journal until the end of my lease on October 31. Each day, I would record how many days were left. Since I had a few months left, I decided that the best way to downsize was to start with the ten percent generally left at the end of packing. Do you know what I am talking about? All the paperwork and odds and ends you do not know what to do with at the end of your move. My friend Ashley calls this the Doom Box.

LORILYN B. ALDEN

As I started to release items, I was overwhelmed. I tried to sell the items I loved on Facebook and discovered that the only person who thought they had value was me. Plus I hated all the back-and-forth and negotiating and arranging meetings with people who did not show up. At one of my girls' tearoom chats with Whitney, I asked her how she would release almost everything she owned. She thought for a moment and then said something profound. She said she would probably invite her friends and family to take what they want. My sacral response agreed.

I love to cook and entertain, so I have all the best kitchen tools. My son and his girlfriend were preparing not only to have my first granddaughter but also to purchase their first home. My son also shared my love of cooking, so it made sense to me to gift them most of my kitchen items. A friend's daughter was turning eighteen and moving into her first apartment, so I gifted her the pink plates I adored.

This way of releasing filled my heart and made it easy for me to let go. Even though I had a studio apartment and considered myself a minimalist, I was amazed at how much stuff I had. I told myself I was wrong when I thought I lacked abundance; it was all around me, but I had taken it for granted. I promised myself that regardless of how long my journey of travel lasted, if I should decide to create a home again, I would be more mindful of what I own.

More sentimental items like all the baskets I had from my mom became easy to release when I saw my friend Robin had posted on Facebook looking for baskets. She was making baskets to give to charities for their raffles, door prizes, etc. I immediately sent her pictures of all my baskets, and she was thrilled to accept them. My mom would have been happy to know her baskets went to good causes.

Anyone who knows me knows I love clothes, shoes, and accessories, even though I did not wear most of my closet. It's said we wear only about ten percent, which I believe has been the case. I had a dear friend who had an unexcepted health challenge, causing her to have to leave her career in the spa industry and seek corporate work again.

Since she was out of work, she had been living on her savings, and with money being tight, she needed to get a new wardrobe for work. I told her to come over and help me downsize my wardrobe because she had great style and could help me eliminate some of my clothes. She left with dresses, pants, tops, coats, shoes, and accessories. I could have donated my clothes to a women's shelter, but this was more personal and meant more. It was a blessing for both of us. She had new clothes for work, and the clothes I loved went to someone I cared deeply about.

My book collection was another challenge to release, but I gave them all to my coach, Colleen. Colleen works with women like me who initially needed help but did not necessarily have the resources to spend hundreds of dollars on coaching. She offers her clients a sliding scale based on their income and situation. She would often loan her books to help her clients learn new skills. I know because she introduced me to a plethora of books on the various topics I needed to learn. I wanted to support her work of helping women and thought she would be the best guardian of my treasured book collection.

The release and planning for my global travel was exciting and scary, but I promised myself that if the excitement outweighed the fear, I would move forward. Each decision made me feel like I was stepping back into my power. Then I got a call from the TEDx organizers I had done my last talk with back in 2021. Yes, the surprise marriage proposal one. They asked me if I would consider doing a talk next February about my communication system, CHAT. Ironically, I had sworn off doing anything with TED. My first reaction in my head was hell no, but because I had retrained myself not to make decisions when I was emotionally charged, I asked if I could think about it and get back to them.

I thought about the opportunity to speak at a TEDx event again, and even though I swore I would never do it again, I liked the idea of taking my power back. The last time I spoke, I felt like the rug had been ripped out from underneath me and all my hard work had gone out the window, overshadowed by a narcissist. As you can see, I also needed to wait for my emotional clarity to make sure I would be doing it for the right reasons, not egotistic ones.

I contacted the organizer and said I would love to take the TEDx stage again, but I had three conditions. First, although talking about my business would be a great opportunity, I wanted a do-over of my last talk that would also include the blind spots and lessoned learned from that experience. Second, I wanted to remove my previous TEDx talk from all TED platforms. When you do a TEDx talk, you sign a waiver saying that you no longer own the content and that it is the property of TED. And third, I wanted the event organizer to person-ally coach me. He is a brilliant and talented storyteller. I respected him professionally and knew he would challenge me to be a better version of myself. He told me he would have to talk to the team and get back to me.

A few days later, he called and told me the team agreed and that due to the special circumstances around my last talk TED had decided to take down my video and that he would coach me! I was filled with emotions. I was excited to take my power back, get on the red carpet again, and deliver the topic I was so passionate about—and for the hindsight's gained from the last experience. Then I felt a huge relief that my previous talk, the thorn in my side, was removed from cyberspace. Part of me was very satisfied that Jack would no longer have a video that painted him as something he was not. Then it hit me: I remembered how much work, time, and energy it takes to do a TEDx talk, and I was about to take that on again.

My vision was becoming a reality as each day passed. Once again, the Universe worked its magic. I wanted to sleep in my bed until the day I left. One day, when texting with my landlord, I had the intuition to share with her that I was looking to sell all my furniture. All my furniture was brand-new; purchased when I'd moved in. She did not acknowledge that text, but several weeks later, my neighbors stopped me when I was leaving to run errands. They said they'd heard I was moving, and at first I was put off. Why would my landlord tell them my personal information? Then they said their daughter was moving from Atlanta to Florida and would like to take my apartment. And they wanted to look at what I was selling rather than paying to move her belongings or purchase new stuff. We walked to my apartment, and they looked around and decided to take all of it. Guess what? Because she was moving in after I moved out, I enjoyed all the benefits of my home until the day I moved out, just as I requested.

A friend told me that I am one of the luckiest people I know. My response was, "Am I lucky, or am I in alignment?" I spent my last few months enjoying every moment of my beach home paradise and quality time with the people I loved. On October 31, when I moved out of my apartment, I went to the beach opening, where it had all started, and once again, I found myself crying with gratitude. I thanked my apartment and the beach for assisting me in my recovery and reclaiming my power. It was time to live my favorite quote by Thoreau: "Go confidently in the direction of your dreams and live the life you always imagined." It was time to step into my power and liberate me. My dream of global travel was becoming my reality.

RESOURCES

For a list of all the books, authors, YouTube channels mentioned in the book, and for additional resources, visit: Manaholic.com/Resources.

I curated a music playlist of my favorite songs to accompany each chapter. Check it out here: www.manaholic.com/playlist.

If you are inspired to take a healing journey of your own and want to dive a little deeper through the intimate relationship of journaling, check out these Journal Prompts: www.manaholic.com/journalprompts.

If you would like to organize a group or book club to read along with, download discussions prompts at: www.manaholic.com/bookclubdiscussions.

Follow my journey on YouTube as I liberate my body, mind, and soul to live my heart's desires as I dance across the globe, meet new people, and explore new cultures.

https://www.youtube.com/@LiberatingLorilyn

ABOUT THE AUTHOR

Lorilyn B. Alden is a global speaker, master facilitator, TEDx speaker, curator, and coach. She is the founder and creator of the CHAT Communication System, an innovative communication-style assessment tool and methodology. Lorilyn has been in front of the camera as a TV host and behind the camera as an award-winning producer. She founded a nonprofit organization that supported teenage girls in building positive self-esteem, healthy boundaries, and goal setting, which was recognized in two national magazines and other media outlets. When not immersed in her professional endeavors, she's out riding motorcycles, salsa dancing, spending quality time with her sons and friends, or satisfying her gypsy soul by traveling.

If you'd like to share your thoughts about the book or have questions, email Lorilyn at info@Manaholic.com.

MEET THE TRIBE

Nancy Butler-Ross, TheBookMuse@aol.com, is a freelance editor, published author, and former *Miami Herald* columnist. She especially enjoys collaborating on books that bring Light to the planet.

Annie Sarac is a freelance editor. You can find out more about her editing services as well as books she's written at TheEditingPen.com.

Brooke Fischer, BrookeFischer.com, grew up in Boulder, Colorado, and studied at the Colorado Institute of Art, Denver. She is a fine art painter and graphic designer. Brooke is a passionate advocate for the environment and equal rights.

Lindsay Samuels is honored to serve as the web designer for Manaholic.com. Lindsay is the founder of Guiding Star Healing Arts (TheGuidingStar.Life), whose mission is helping others to align with their own inner compass and fulfill their life's purpose.

CHAT ASSESSMENT

Below are the instructions and onetime access code to a complimentary CHAT Assessment.

- Go to TheChatSystem.com
- Click on the CHAT Assessment tab (mobile users scroll down the menu to the bottom)
- Read the instructions and tips
- Click "add to cart"
- Add coupon code: Manaholic
- Apply coupon
- Proceed to checkout
- Add your name and email
- Place order
- Click "take the assessment here"

When you take the assessment, you will receive immediate on-screen results and an email report (check your spam folder).

The complimentary CHAT assessment will automatically sign you up for our monthly newsletter. If you prefer not to receive the monthly email, use the unsubscribe button at the bottom of your report.

If your results don't resonate with you, please use the Contact button to schedule a complimentary fifteen-minute consultation to clarify any questions you may have.

Lorilyn B. Alden

Are you looking for a dynamic and authentic speaker for your next event? Are you a woman who does not feel heard, struggles with your boundaries, and desires to speak your truth? Lorilyn provides coaching, communities, and retreats to support you on your journey to reconnect with your voice, speak your truth, and stand courageously in your authenticity.

To work with Lorilyn, visit lorilynbalden.com or email info@lorilyn balden.com.

Collaborate with Lorilyn to keynote at your next event or to customize effective communication training with your team.

Visit www.thechatsystem.com or email info@thechatsystem.com.

COMING SOON

Manaholic is a trilogy collection.

Be on the lookout for the release of

Manaholic: Liberated.